CONCERT PROGRAMMES IN THE UK AND IRELAND

Concert Programmes in the UK and Ireland

A Preliminary Report

Rupert Ridgewell

IAML(UK & Irl) and the Music Libraries Trust
London 2003

Published jointly by the International Association of Music Libraries, Archives and Documentation Centres: United Kingdom and Irland Branch and the Music Libraries Trust

First published 2003.

Printed in Great Britain on acid-free paper by Driftgate Press, Aylesbury

ISBN 0-952-07039-1

Contents

Preface

In 2000 The Music Libraries Trust drew up a list of projects that it wished to foster and encourage. At the top of this list it placed the idea of a union catalogue of concert programmes in the UK and Ireland, which it saw as an essential tool for scholars, researchers and music librarians. It was thought appropriate to begin with a scoping study to bring together what was already known and to examine how such a project might be taken further. Rupert Ridgewell of the British Library Music Collections agreed to take it on. What Dr Ridgewell produced went far beyond his modest brief and the Trust felt that his report, with its extensive lists, was so useful as to warrant publication as an interim measure before any larger project might get underway. Dr Ridgewell kindly agreed to further additions to his report, including an index, and all that was needed to turn a report into a book.

The Trust is grateful to Dr Ridgewell for the immense amount of hard work that he has put into this. The Trust would also like to thank members of the Concert Programmes Working Party (Chris Banks, Paul Banks, Christina Bashford and Lewis Foreman) for their help, advice and contribution to the project, IAML (UK & Ireland) for its willingness to act as co-publisher and its Publications Officer, Margaret Roll, for her energy, enthusiasm and common sense in dealing with the book's publication and promotion.

John Tyrrell
Chair, The Music Libraries Trust

Introduction

Concert programmes remain the Cinderellas of music information retrieval in the UK and Ireland. For many years, music librarians and researchers have been aware of the difficulties of finding out what programmes exist, where they are held and what their contents are. Despite being recognised as a primary source for historical and musicological research, they have never been systematically documented at a national or regional level. Collections of programmes, large and small, wide-ranging or very specific, are to be found in libraries, public archives, collections of music societies and concert venues, and in numerous private collections. Finding the details of one concert, or of performances of one work across a range of concerts, is time-consuming or simply impossible.

This report stems from a project carried out for the Music Libraries Trust in 2002. It aims both to define the scope of a union catalogue of concert programmes in the UK and Ireland and to reaffirm the importance of concert programmes as a unique documentary record of musical life over the past three centuries. Chapters 1 and 2 describe the significance of concert programmes as a research resource and the problems associated with locating them, while Chapter 3 attempts an overview of the resource. The report also draws together information about related projects that document programmes or the information contained within them (in Chapter 4). Some of the problems involved with describing, cataloguing and conserving a representative collection are outlined in Chapter 5. This knowledge informs the recommendations for future work given in Chapters 6 and 7.

The preliminary register of holdings, given in the appendices, gives details of collections held by 150 institutions. Collections range from long runs of programmes of major concert series and venues, to individual items interspersed within otherwise unrelated archives. The register nevertheless represents merely the tip of the iceberg as far as UK and

Irish holdings are concerned. Many collections remain to be uncovered, but it is hoped that this preliminary work will provide the impetus for a larger project to document all significant sources of concert programmes archived in the UK and Ireland, with a view to improving access to them and ensuring their long-term preservation.

Rupert Ridgewell
London, June 2003

Acknowledgements

The report would not have been possible without the generosity of countless individuals who provided information about collections of concert programmes in their institutions. Whilst it is impossible to mention everyone in the space available, I would like to express my thanks in particular to Geraldine Auerbach (Jewish Music Institute), Duncan Barker (*Making Music*), Derek Bartley (Rhyl Music Club), Peter Baxter (Edinburgh City Libraries), Almut Boehme (National Library of Scotland), Brian Clark (Dundee Central Library), Emma Costello (National Library of Ireland), Oliver Davies (Royal College of Music), Robert Flower (Cockermouth Harmonic Society), Marian Hogg (Trinity College of Music), Beresford King-Smith (City of Birmingham Symphony Orchestra), Bridget Palmer (Royal Academy of Music), Roy Stanley (Trinity College, Dublin), and Tony Trowles (Westminster Abbey).

I am indebted to various people who contributed to the report in other ways: Paul Andrews and Katharine Hogg alerted me to new collection records in *Cecilia* that mentioned programmes; Chris Banks, Nicolas Bell and Ian Davis helped to track down British Library collections; and Paul Banks, David Day, Jenny Doctor, Arthur Searle, and William Weber provided information about the projects described in Chapter 4.

For commenting on earlier drafts of the report, I owe a great debt of gratitude to Christina Bashford, Oliver Davies, Mark De Novellis, Lewis Foreman, and Arthur Searle. The report would not have reached its present form without the support, guidance and encouragement of Professor John Tyrrell and the Music Libraries Trust.

1. The Research Resource

Definitions

Concert programmes have changed radically over the course of the last 250 years. The earliest printed programmes were little more than handbills, distributed in advance of a concert with a listing of the works and performers. There were no explanatory notes or biographies, features that are essential to programmes today, and the programme was printed on one sheet of paper. Word-books were commonly produced for vocal recitals or oratorio performances in the eighteenth and nineteenth centuries. They contained the words (or complete libretti) of vocal works and functioned as programmes in their own right. Programmes began to include explanatory material only in the second half of the nineteenth century, when it became common for them to incorporate descriptions of works, illustrations, and even extracts from the scores. They acquired an explanatory, educational function and grew in size to become small booklets, available at a price. Later in the twentieth century, the programme was used to promote other concerts, the careers of performers, and to advertise products by sponsoring companies.

This development broadly reflects the changing nature of musical life and the social function of the concert over the same period. In the eighteenth century, formal concerts were typically patronized by members of the aristocracy and upper middle classes. As music became increasingly accessible to a wider section of society after 1800, the concert acquired a didactic function, supporting the emergence of a canon of musical works. Concert programmes therefore began to include detailed analytical and historical notes that described and evaluated the music being performed.

In the last one hundred years, concerts have increasingly attracted sponsorship from commercial organisations and their content has been defined increasingly by the demands of the record industry. The concert programme became the means by which these organisations could market themselves to the concert-going public. As the importance of the performer became paramount, and programmes began to include biographies and photographs of performers, they have become objects of desire, and subsequently highly prized and collectable.[1] However, the defining elements of the programme have not changed: it remains by nature an ephemeral item, defined by its association with a specific event in time, and its key function is to guide an audience through a concert by listing the music being performed.

In the preceding discussion I have deliberately adhered to a rather simple definition of the terms 'concert' and 'programme'. Since I refer here to concert music in the western classical tradition, my definition of a 'concert programme' is narrowly focused by association with the types of events that we now commonly associate with concert halls, whether chamber or orchestral in dimension. The scope can clearly be widened to include other types of musical event, such as pop, rock, folk or jazz concerts, or theatrical genres like operas, musicals, or ballets. In many cases, programmes for each type of event may be preserved in miscellaneous collections assembled by an avid concertgoer with an eclectic taste in music. Such collections are commonly acquired by music libraries from private individuals and often present unique material as well as their own problems of classification. A typical collection is described in Chapter 5 of this report. They may also include programmes of events with a high musical content that would not be identified as concerts. Religious services are a prime example.

Music forms an integral part of worship for many denominations and services may include hymns, psalms, anthems, and settings of liturgical texts. On some occasions music may even constitute the focal point of the proceedings, requiring the distribution of a special service sheet. Plate 1 reproduces a page from the service sheet for the Purcell

---

[1]This process began in the nineteenth century, albeit for educational reasons. For discussion of programme collecting in the nineteenth century, see Christina Bashford, 'Not Just 'G.': Towards a History of the Programme Note', in *George Grove, Music and Victorian Culture*, ed. Michael Musgrave (London: Palgrave Macmillan, 2003)

Commemoration at Westminster Abbey on 21 November 1895, marking the 200th anniversary of the composer's death. The service was held to inaugurate an appeal for a new case for the organ at Westminster Abbey and included a selection of Purcell anthems conducted by John Stainer, Arthur Sullivan and Frederick Bridge. The 'service sheet' for this event – in reality a booklet published by Novello, Ewer & Co., complete with illustrations for the design of the organ case – appears in the British Library Catalogue of Printed Music under Purcell's name and with a uniform title stating simply 'Programmes. London, Westminster Abbey' (see Plate 1). It seems appropriate to class this particular item as a programme, given the high musical content and the historical importance of the event, but what of service sheets for occasions that did not have such a direct musical association? Prescribing a sensible division here between different types of service, depending on their musical content, is difficult to achieve.

Stretching the definition further, it is entirely possible to take a somewhat wider view of what constitutes a 'concert programme'. Programme information may by gleaned from a variety of primary sources and not only from the material distributed at a concert. Flyers or posters may yield a wealth of information about a concert, such as the works to be performed, names of performers, ticket prices, promotional details and iconographical information. In cases where the actual programme has not survived, this type of material can be especially valuable. Secondary sources may also provide details of programme content. The music listings of the *Radio Times* include detailed information about concerts in the UK in the second half of the twentieth century, even if they are secondary to the programmes produced for the concerts themselves. Similarly, the short-lived series of quarterly BBC Music Programmes (designed to advertise forthcoming concert broadcasts on the Third Programme) are useful sources for investigating the history of music broadcasting, but they cannot be classed as primary sources for the history of musical performance.

UNDER THE PATRONAGE OF
THE QUEEN'S MOST EXCELLENT MAJESTY.
H.I.M. THE EMPRESS FREDERICK OF GERMANY.
H.R.H. THE PRINCE OF WALES, K.G.
H.R.H. THE PRINCESS OF WALES.
H.R.H. THE DUKE OF SAXE-COBURG AND GOTHA, K.G.
(DUKE OF EDINBURGH).
H.R.H. THE PRINCESS CHRISTIAN.

PURCELL COMMEMORATION

IN

Westminster Abbey

ON

THURSDAY, NOVEMBER 21, 1895, AT 3 P.M.

BEING THE 200TH ANNIVERSARY OF THE DEATH OF

HENRY PURCELL

Organist of Westminster Abbey (1680-1695)

One of the Organists of the Chapel Royal
and
Composer in Ordinary to His Majesty (1682).

PRINTED BY NOVELLO, EWER AND CO.,
1, BERNERS STREET, LONDON, W.

Pl. 1.
Service sheet for the Purcell Commemoration, Westminster Abbey, 21 November 1895.
The British Library e.1395.a.(4.). Reproduced by permission of the BL Board.

For the purposes of this report I have taken a broad view of what constitutes a concert programme and have included a range of material in Appendix 1. A more limited definition may, however, be necessary to narrow the scope of a union catalogue of programmes and should inform the planning process at an early stage.[2]

Potential value

Historical research

Music historians are increasingly recognising the value of concert programmes as sources of information relevant to the social history of music and as artefacts worthy of study in their own right. Concert programmes are primary source materials for charting the emergence of repertories and the development of musical taste over a period of time. Recent studies of London and Viennese concert life in the late eighteenth and early nineteenth centuries, for example, have explored the institutional and social context of the concert and the reception of particular composers, such as Mozart and Beethoven.[3] Other scholars have chosen a narrower focus, to study the significance and organisation of individual concert institutions, such as the Philharmonic Society or Crystal Palace in London or the Bournemouth Municipal Orchestra and its conductor Dan Godfrey.[4]

The comparative study of concert programmes from different institutions is another area that has gained ground in recent years. This

---

[2]A union catalogue may constitute either a directory of collections or a catalogue of individual items. Practical problems associated with each possibility are considered in Chapters 6 and 7.

[3]Simon McVeigh, *Concert Life in London from Mozart to Haydn* (Cambridge: Cambridge University Press, 1993); Mary Sue Morrow, *Concert Life in Haydn's Vienna: Aspects of a Developing Musical and Social Institution* 'Sociology of Music 7' (Stuyvesant, NY: Pendragon Press, 1988).

[4]Cyril Ehrlich, *First Philharmonic: A History of the Royal Philharmonic Society* (Oxford: Clarendon Press, 1995); Michael Musgrave, *The Musical Life of the Crystal Palace* (Cambridge: Cambridge University Press, 1995); Stephen Lloyd, *Sir Dan Godfrey, Champion of British Composers: a chronology of forty years' music-making with the Bournemouth Municipal Orchestra* (London: Thames Publishing, 1995)

approach involves a systematic analysis of empirical data drawn from concert programmes to investigate broader questions about emerging musical repertoires.[5] A union catalogue of concert programmes will greatly facilitate this type of research, by providing a central point from which to trace extant copies of programmes of particular institutions. It will also assist historians of provincial musical life, by enabling them to locate the history of a music club or choral society in the context of its time, or trace the performances of local composers that were put on further afield.[6] Founded in 1867, the Cockermouth Harmonic Society is one of the oldest established country choirs still active in the UK. Robert Flower is writing the choir's history based on its programmes and coverage of its concerts in the press, but notes the absence of a more general overview of the amateur choral scene from the 1860s onwards. As he says, a union catalogue of programmes will help researchers to locate relevant material and facilitate comparisons between the repertoires of different choirs.[7]

Programmes are important sources of information for biographies of composers and performers,[8] and often include significant scholarly articles from the late nineteenth century, such as essays by composers on the occasion of a first performance. They can also provide primary evidence for studying the creative process. The initial performing version of the slow movement of Brahms's first symphony, for example, has been

---

[5]The work carried out by William Weber is representative of this approach. See in particular his article 'Miscellany vs. Homogeneity: Concert Programmes at the Royal Academy of Music and the Royal College of Music in the 1880s', in *Music and British Culture, 1785-1914: Essays in Honour of Cyril Ehrlich*, ed. Christina Bashford and Leanne Langley (Oxford: Oxford University Press, 2000), 299-320.

[6]Histories of the Broadheath Singers and the Slaithwaite Philharmonic Orchestra have been derived largely from sets of old programmes. See *Before Elgar... and after: 25 years of the Broadheath Singers*, edited by David J. Brown (Iver Heath: The Broadheath Singers, 1995); Adrian Smith, *An improbable centenary: the life and times of the Slaithwaite Philharmonic orchestra 1891-1990* (Huddersfield: Slaithwaite Philharmonic Orchestral Society, 1990)

[7]Robert Flower, personal communication.

[8]Philippe Autexier examines programmes of recitals given by Franz Liszt to show that Liszt did not seek to 'educate' his public, but tried to accommodate their culture and interests in his selection of pieces. See Philippe Autexier, 'Musique sans frontière? Les choix des programmes de Liszt pour ses concerts de la période virtuose', *La Revue Musicale*, 405-07 (1987), 297-305.

reconstructed from contemporary programme notes and extant manuscript string parts.[9] Brahms made substantial changes to the movement after its first performances, transforming the original rondo form into a ternary form by relocating substantial sections of music. These changes have interesting implications for understanding Brahms's compositional processes as well as for analysing the movement.

Other elements of the programme, such as illustrative material or advertisements, may provide valuable information. Pamela Poulin has been able to reconstruct details of Anton Stadler's basset clarinet (made by Theodor Lotz) from engravings that were included in his concert programmes in Riga during February and March 1794.[10] She discusses the design of the instrument and its relation to the basset horn, with reference to the music performed in these concerts – including Mozart's clarinet concerto, K. 622.

Scholars have also studied concert programmes in their own right, recognising them as emblems of ideology and embodiments of perceptions of musical taste. Jann Pasler, for example, examines Parisian programmes for the period between 1890 and 1914. These programmes document a series of radical transformations in the ways that music was presented to the public and in how the French thought about music. As Pasler writes:

> ...the notes, cover imagery, typefaces, and advertisements reveal a gradual repudiation of one form of modernism during this period – modernism associated with feminine imagery, art nouveau design, and Beauty with a capital B. Adopted in its place was a more male-oriented, abstract modernism, valued for embodying the new'.[11]

Concert programmes can also aid the dating and cataloguing of

---

[9]Robert Pascall, 'Brahms's first symphony slow movement: the initial performing version', *Musical Times*, 122 (October 1981), 664-67.

[10]Pamela L. Poulin, 'Anton Stadler's basset clarinet: Recent discoveries in Riga', *Journal of the American Musical Instrument Society* 22 (1996), 110-27.

[11]Jann Pasler, 'Concert programs and their narratives as emblems of ideology', *International Journal of Musicology* 2 (1993), 249-308.

manuscript scores or parts. Copies of Philharmonic Society programmes, for example, have been used to date manuscripts of works performed by the society and preserved in its archive, now held by the British Library.[12]

It is hard not to conclude that concert programmes represent a potential goldmine of information for the music researcher, a goldmine that has remained relatively inaccessible owing to the lack of any effective tools to facilitate resource discovery.

Lifelong learning and enjoyment

Ephemera is a term used to embrace a wide range of minor, everyday documents and artefacts, most intended for one-time or short term use. Items that fall into this category were created to meet an immediate need, usually transitory in nature, and they were not intended to be saved. The value of such mundane items today owes much to the fact that they are elusive and because they offer a unique window into the everyday realities of life for previous generations. Collecting ephemeral paper items first became widespread during the Victorian era when such objects as trade cards and greeting cards were accumulated to paste into scrap albums.[13] Today, ephemeral objects are increasingly used by libraries as a tool for stimulating interest among remote users in their collections, as witnessed by the recent revival of interest in popular sheet music of the nineteenth century. The digitisation of Victorian song sheets forms part of a number of recent and on-going projects: among them, the Broadside Ballads project at the Bodleian Library and *A sense of place* at the British Library. The Library of Congress also has a Printed Ephemera Collection available electronically, which highlights broadsides and other items in the library's collections.

Programmes are ephemeral in the sense that they are produced in the first instance to guide members of an audience through a musical event. This practical purpose obviously loses its relevance once the concert is

---

[12]Arthur Searle, Honorary Librarian, Royal Philharmonic Society, personal communication.

[13]See Maurice Rickards and Michael Twyman (ed.), *The Encyclopedia of ephemera: a guide to the fragmentary documents of everyday life for the collector, curator and historian* (New York: Routledge, 2000)

over, although many people retain their programmes as a souvenir of a memorable occasion for future reference. Concert programmes may therefore be used as a powerful tool to stimulate interest in music history, the social function of concerts in earlier periods, and the development of musical tastes from the seventeenth and eighteenth centuries to the present day. The general music lover will find much to identify with in the documentation of concert activity in earlier times, perhaps especially if it relates to a performing venue or ensemble that is still active.

Economic value

A survey of holding institutions would also make it easier to determine which programmes are lost, or held only by one or two institutions. This will enable librarians to determine which programmes to collect and preserve, based upon the holdings of other institutions, and have a major impact on national collection development. Several librarians and curators who have been in contact during the course of this study have described the problems they currently face when presented with a miscellaneous collection of concert programmes, often by donation. It is often impossible to determine whether individual programmes are unique or held elsewhere. The dilemma that many librarians face, therefore, is whether to accept large collections and devote the time needed to weed and catalogue them, given limited resources and no reliable method to find out which programmes should be preserved. The availability of a union catalogue of concert programmes will therefore make a positive impact on library budgets, by saving time and resources spent on selection, cataloguing and preservation.

A union catalogue will also serve to increase the monetary value of some programmes that might be deemed rare or especially important. There is a clear market for programmes that appeal to devotees of particular artists, groups or composers, as may be seen in the catalogues of antiquarian dealers and auction houses. In a recent catalogue, the dealer Lisa Cox offered four concert and ballet programmes for sale. Prices ranged from £30 for an unsigned programme of a recital by the pianist Nikita

Magaloff, to £175 for a signed programme of a concert given by Peter Pears and Benjamin Britten in Birmingham in 1954.[14] At the other end of the spectrum, programmes can be picked up at ephemera fairs and in music dealers ephemera trays, often at very reasonable prices.

Concert programmes for pop and rock concerts are also becoming increasingly collectable. Pop concert programmes come in two main varieties: 'tour' programmes that are produced for every concert on an artist's tour and individual 'gig' programmes which commemorate just one concert or special event. Of the two types, the latter are the more scarce and consequently the more valuable. According to Collector Cafe – an internet-based forum for collectors and dealers covering a wide range of subjects – gig programmes can sell for between $10 and over $300 depending on the artist and period. Programmes from the Beatles UK tours in 1963, 1964 and 1965, for example, might sell for $300 or more in mint condition.[15] The value of a programme will inevitably be enhanced if a survey of holding institutions in the UK and Ireland indicates that no other copies are preserved.

---

[14] Lisa Cox Music, catalogue *Gallimaufray 8*, items 29 and 92. See: http://www.lisacoxmusic.com/

[15] See http://www.collectorcafe.com/

2. Finding Programmes

Preliminary Register of Collections

The results of this preliminary survey show that concert programmes are preserved in archives, libraries and museums in many different contexts in the UK and Ireland. Information gathered during the course of the study is summarised in Appendix 1, which is arranged alphabetically by location. It should be stressed that the register does not represent a comprehensive listing of all major institutions. Rather, the aim is to demonstrate the breadth of material preserved across various domains and the different contexts in which programmes are to be found. It is expected that the list will form the starting point for any future project to document the field.

The information was gathered in three ways. In the first instance, a press release and invitation to contribute to the study was issued and awareness of the project was raised by the publication of articles in national music magazines and specialist periodicals. These included *Classical Music*, *Musical Opinion*, *Making Music News*, the *IAML(UK & Irl) Newsletter*, the *AMARC Newsletter*, and the *Newsletter of the Cathedral Libraries and Archives Association.*[1] The feedback from these announcements was good, with many potential collaborators expressing enthusiasm for the project and offering information about their collections. The response from individuals associated with private archives and music societies was especially encouraging.

---

[1]The author also gave presentations about the project at the AGM of the Cathedral Libraries and Archives Association (London 2002), at the IAML(UK & Irl) Annual Study Weekend, (Durham 2002), and at the inaugural meeting of Orchestral Archivists (Birmingham 2003).

Secondly, the survey coincided with the realisation of a number of information retrieval projects in the humanities, some of which led to the creation of new descriptions of programme collections, or of archive collections that include programmes. Data was gathered from the *Archives Hub*, the *Access to Archives* (A2A) database, *Backstage* (a performing arts gateway for the UK), and SIBMAS (the International Directory of Performing Arts Collections and Institutions). The survey also coincided with the initial data-gathering phase of the *Cecilia* project, which gave a broad indication of the numbers of music libraries (especially) that hold concert ephemera, albeit without providing detailed information about holdings in most cases.[1]

The third method of collecting information, inevitably, was by word-of-mouth, and I am particularly grateful to Christina Bashford and Lewis Foreman for alerting me to numerous important collections.

Collections of programmes held by the British Library and by the National Libraries of Scotland and Ireland have been treated separately and are listed in Appendix 2 and 3 respectively. It is hoped that the three appendices combined will give locations of runs of programmes for many of the significant venues and ensembles. The index is designed primarily to aid searching the appendices and includes entries for personal names, venues (listed by location), and titles of concert series (under individual titles and the heading 'concert series').

Search Strategies

How would one go about finding a collection of programmes, or an individual programme, not listed in the register? Much research is often required to access material in different types of institution and even across departments in a single institution, but this will vary depending on the nature of the query. For existing venues, ensembles or music festivals, an obvious port of call will be the organisation itself (although their collections may not always be readily accessible). The City of Birmingham Symphony Orchestra, for example, has a collection of 'check' programmes that were

[1]The form for contributors included a check box to indicate the presence of concert programmes in a collection.

annotated by the orchestra manager with timings and any changes of artist or programme.[2] In some cases sets of programmes may be scattered across several different collections, none of which offer a complete run. For example, there are no complete sets of Crystal Palace programmes, but there are substantial runs at the British Library, Royal Academy of Music, Royal College of Music and the Henry Watson Music Library.

Local studies archives are a vital source for concert ephemera. In many cases they have extensive historical collections relating to local events, although their collections are rarely catalogued at item level or made available via public catalogues. They may, however, be filed in a chronological order or into concert series sequence, which obviously makes it easier to locate a programme for a particular concert, where the date of the concert is known.

Finding the programme of a concert that featured a particular performer or work clearly presents a greater challenge, although a few institutions have developed finding aids tailor-made for this type of enquiry. The most important example is the RCM Department of Portraits and Performance History, which maintains card indexes for artists, first performances, orchestra lists, subscriber lists and iconographical content. Finding aids compiled by a private collector may also prove useful if the collection's integrity is maintained. Myra Hess's collection of National Gallery programmes, now held by the British Library, is a case in point. It includes a catalogue of works performed in the series (compiled by Harold Ferguson), an index of performers, and a notebook listing dates of first performances (see Appendix 2, London - National Gallery Concerts).

Major gaps in the coverage certainly exist, even of concert series that are still active. Copies of the programme for the third Aldeburgh Festival (1950), for example, are especially scarce. Researchers may have to resort to alternative sources of information, such as newspaper reviews, posters and flyers, to reconstruct an event. For some major societies or festivals, published indexes may provide relevant information: Rosamund Strode's

[2]Timings may determine the pay for rank-and-file players. This practice has a long history: Sir George Smart, for example, annotated programmes of his concerts with meticulous care during the nineteenth century.

Music of Forty Festivals is de facto an index to the music played at the first forty Aldeburgh Festivals; other notable examples are Myles Birket Foster's history of the Philharmonic Society and Anthony Boden's history of the Three Choirs Festival.[3]

Library catalogues

Describing a concert programme and making it accessible via printed or online catalogues represents a peculiar challenge, one that librarians have solved in a variety of ways without reaching any general consensus about how it should be achieved. The two key defining elements of concert programmes are the time and place of a live event, elements that library cataloguers are accustomed to include within the bibliographical record. Indeed, there is no specific provision for them in *Anglo-American Cataloguing Rules*. The only instructions regarding the treatment of events appear in the chapter relating to corporate bodies in AACR2 (section 21.1B1, p.313). Here, the rules state that ad hoc events (such as athletic contests, exhibitions, expeditions, fairs and festivals) are to be considered as corporate bodies. This is how many programmes are treated in library catalogues.

As a result, concert programmes may be catalogued under a variety of different headings and organised according to concert location, collector, venue, performer, composer, orchestra, or concert series. This lack of consistency is in itself a barrier to effective resource discovery. There is also a degree of inconsistency in the way that concert programmes are described, which should be taken into account when interrogating online catalogues in particular. Thus concert programmes may be described as 'recital programme', 'programme notes', 'programmes of music', or similar formulations.

---

[3]Rosamund Strode, *Music of Forty Festivals: a list of works performed at Aldeburgh Festivals from 1948 to 1987* (Aldeburgh: Aldeburgh Foundation, 1987); Myles Birket Foster, *History of the Philharmonic Society of London: 1813-1912* (London: John Lane Bell, 1912); Anthony Boden, *Three Choirs: A History of the Festival* (London: Allan Sutton, 1992).

Making the situation worse, the ephemeral nature of the programme is reflected in the way they are treated. Large collections of miscellaneous concert programmes are rarely catalogued at item level, but are subsumed within a single 'dump' entry (see Chapter 3). Such entries rarely function effectively as collection-level records and offer no effective control over the collection from a management perspective. The material remains 'hidden' from the view of potential users.

In some cases programmes were paginated consecutively from concert to concert to make up annual volumes. This applies to several late nineteenth orchestral societies such as the (Royal) Liverpool Philharmonic and the Hallé, and to choral festivals such as the Birmingham Triennial Festival. Such collections can be legitimately treated as serials, with a single catalogue entry for the entire run, and a note of any gaps.

Another barrier to finding programmes is the lack of any higher level finding aid or directory of collections of concert programmes within most institutions. The searching tools – catalogues, indexes and other finding aids – are, in many cases, incomplete, with the result that a reduced level of service is provided. The fact that a variety of catalogues and indexes have to be searched is both a disincentive to casual users and an annoyance to dedicated users.

At the British Library most collections of London concert programmes are entered in the general library catalogue under the heading 'LONDON III. Miscellaneous Institutions, Societies, and other Bodies', or under the name of the venue or concert society. Individual programmes catalogued in recent years also tend to be entered under the title, with varying levels of detail included in the title page transcription. It is essential to check catalogues of special collections within the library, such as the *Catalogue of Printed Music to 1980*, where a large number of collections are entered under the heading 'Programmes'. Concert programmes have sometimes been kept with the manuscript archives to which they relate. These tend to be miscellaneous collections relating to an individual, such as an agent or performer, or archives of a performing group or venue. They are listed in Appendix 2 under the title of the collection or the name associated with the collection. Further details may be obtained from the library's Manuscripts Online Catalogue (http://molcat.bl.uk).[1]

[1]A useful partial listing is given in Alec Hyatt King, *A Wealth of Music in the British Library (Reference Collection) and the British Museum* (London: Clive Bingley, 1983), 108-10.

3. Collections

How many collections of programmes are there in the UK and Ireland? To what extent do they overlap one another and where are the important gaps in coverage? Full answers to these questions await a more systematic survey of the resource, but the listing in the appendices to this study makes it possible to gain a broad overview of the resource for the first time. In this chapter, I shall draw together the various strands of information to give an indication of the number of collections in each sector, their approximate size and the degree of overlap between them. I shall focus especially upon one or two examples from each sector.

Copyright libraries

Within the terms of the Copyright Act 1911, a 'publisher' is to be understood as anyone who issues or distributes publications to the public. Items published in the United Kingdom and in Ireland are liable for deposit, as are items originally published elsewhere but distributed in the United Kingdom and in Ireland. The requirement for deposit remains, irrespective of the place of publication or printing, the nature and size of the imprint, or the extent of its distribution. Programmes for public concerts clearly fall within these parameters, in that they are distributed and made available to an audience drawn from the general public. Private concerts and concerts given at schools and colleges, however, would normally not be liable for deposit.

In theory, concert programmes, along with similar types of printed ephemera, are covered by legal deposit and should be routinely submitted to the BL and to the other five copyright libraries. In reality very few organisations regularly deposit material with these institutions, and the libraries themselves have not committed the resources to tackling the problem in any systematic way. In part this is because of the very nature of the product: programmes distributed at one concert venue are very often not published by the venue itself, or by any single printer or publisher. Each individual ensemble may make its own arrangements, or a sponsor, agent, or promoter of the event may produce the programme. Thus responsibility for depositing a programme does not rest on the shoulders of any one individual and the venue itself may not be in a position to insist on the deposit of material (although several venues maintain their own archives, as discussed below).

There is also a lack of strategic focus. The collecting of concert programmes has not been formalised as such by the Standing Committee on Legal Deposit (SCOLD, comprising all six libraries) and the libraries have not co-ordinated their collection development policies. Individual libraries endeavour to collect programmes from their local area – the Bodleian Library, for example, covers Oxford and the surrounding area – but there is no strategy in place to ensure the preservation of a national distributed collection, in which relevant material is collected by libraries on a regional basis. The result is that the gaps in the collections far outweigh the coverage.

British Library

The British Library's collections of concert programmes are international in scope and cover the widest period, from the seventeenth century to the present day. The coverage includes programmes of events not only in the UK and Ireland, but also in Australia, Austria, Colombia, France, Germany, Holland, Italy, Mexico, the USA, and other countries. Concert programmes are preserved in various different parts of the library – in the Music Library, General Humanities Collections, Early Printed Collections, and the Department of Manuscripts – which means that readers are obliged to search various catalogues to gain access to material. This problem has been eased somewhat with the appearance of the BL's integrated catalogue portal at http://blpc.bl.uk, although the manuscripts catalogue remains separate.

The collections as a whole encompass some 7000 individual programmes catalogued separately, plus over 300 collections of uncatalogued programmes that are accessible only via 'dump' entries in the catalogues. It is impossible to give a precise figure for the size of the uncatalogued backlogs, although at a conservative estimate (assuming an average of 100 items per collection) this may be in the region of 300,000 programmes. It should be noted, however, that a number of collections comprise many thousands of individual items, so the total is likely to be higher.[1] Depending on the nature of the collection, a 'dump' entry may appear in the catalogue under the concert location or name of the collector, or indeed under a bland collective title such as 'Collection of programmes'. One such miscellaneous collection of programmes is discussed in Chapter 5, while a summary listing of collections held by the British Library is given in Appendix 2. Individual programmes are typically catalogued under the location or name of the venue or promoting body.

For similar reasons, the BL collections present significant problems associated with collection development. There is currently no way of finding out where the gaps in the collections are, apart from checking the shelves, and the library has not committed the resources to establish a strategy for collecting and preserving concert ephemera.

Bodleian Library

The Music Section maintains collections of posters and programmes of local concerts from the Holywell Music Room concerts of the eighteenth century to the present day. It also holds the collection of opera programmes of Harold Rosenthal, the late founder and editor of *Opera* magazine. They are arranged by opera title, so that programmes relating to different productions of a particular opera are kept together. Although British productions predominate, there are also many foreign programmes. Many include press cuttings relating to the productions.

The John Johnson Collection is one of the most important collections of printed ephemera in the world. It was assembled by John de Monins Johnson between *ca.*1923 and 1956 and was housed at the Oxford

---

[1]This figure also exludes many thousands of items in the library's collections of miscellaneous playbills (see the introduction to Appendix 2).

University Press until its transfer to the Bodleian Library in 1968. Johnson collected retrospectively, establishing 1939 as his *terminus post quem*, although there are exceptions – the collection of Royal Festival Hall programmes, for example, covers the period from 1951 to 1960. The majority of material dates from the eighteenth, nineteenth and early twentieth centuries. The concert programmes are arranged according to venue in fifteen boxes. The coverage of London venues is most significant, with an impressive selection of programmes from smaller venues of the nineteenth century. There is a degree of overlap here with BL collections – especially with the major venues such as the Royal Festival Hall and Queen's Hall – and with the BBC's Written Archives Centre at Caversham, but a large proportion of the Johnson collection is likely to be unique.

Some important sets of concert and opera programmes have entries in the main library catalogues. These include runs of concert programmes of music societies for Pembroke College (1865–1922), Exeter College (1864 onwards), Keble College (1882 onwards), Jesus College (1885–1920), and Merton College (1862–64, 1883–99), as well as the Oxford Orchestral Association (1886–99) and the Oxford Choral and Philharmonic Society (1869–95). The catalogues also have entries for some single programmes from the UK and around the world.

National Library of Scotland

The National Library of Scotland collects programmes for major musical events in Scotland, such as the Edinburgh International Festival of Music and Drama, and has significant collections of programmes in the Music Special Collections and general humanities collections. The information given in Appendix 3 is based on a search of the library's online catalogue.[2] This yielded records for some 24 collections of programmes and about 50 individual items catalogued separately. Among the collections are near-complete runs for the Edinburgh Festival, the BBC Proms, the BBC Symphony Orchestra, and (surprisingly) the Musashino

[2] I am grateful to Almut Boehme for providing this information.

Ongaku Daigaku of Tokyo, as well as partial runs of programmes for several musical societies, including the Glasgow Choral Union, the Middlesbrough Musical Union, and the Sunderland Philharmonic Society. Several special collections also contain programmes: these include the collection of the Edinburgh Society of Musicians, the Balfour Handel Collection, the Hopkinson Berlioz Collection and Hopkinson Verdi Collection. The library also maintains a collection of diaries and programmes of events at the Queen's Hall, Edinburgh, but it apparently does not have a collection of concert programmes for that venue.

Trinity College Dublin

Trinity College Dublin holds programmes of some major performing institutions, such as the Royal Opera House. In general, however, the coverage is apparently even patchier than the other copyright libraries.[3] The National Library of Ireland, however, has a substantial collection of programmes of Irish venues (for a partial listing, see Appendix 3).[4]

National Library of Wales

The National Library of Wales maintains a comprehensive collection of current Welsh National Opera programmes (catalogued separately), and programmes for every International Concert Season at St. David's Hall and for the BBC National Orchestra of Wales from 1992. The library also collects programmes of performances mounted by English National Opera and the Royal Opera (both from 1986 onwards) and some miscellaneous programmes, which are catalogued separately. Overall, the library's holdings do not appear to be comprehensive of concert activity in Wales, although it may have some uncatalogued collections.

Music Conservatories

Music conservatoire libraries are important repositories of material relating to events promoted by the conservatoires themselves and several

---

[3]Roy Stanley, personal communication.

[4] I am grateful to Emma Costello for providing this information

also preserve programmes of events not directly connected with the institution (these are often acquired from the archives of former teachers or students). The Royal Scottish Academy of Music and Drama library, for example, holds uncatalogued programmes of operas performed in Glasgow and London and programmes for a few Glasgow concerts dating from around 1900. Many programmes from the RSAMD and its predecessor institutions (from 1847) are preserved in the archives of Strathclyde and Glasgow universities.

The Royal College of Music's Department of Portraits and Performance History holds by far the largest archive of programmes. Founded by Sir Keith Falkner and the present Keeper in 1971, the Department was conceived as a specialist offshoot from the RCM Reference Library and pioneered a comprehensive approach to programme collecting and information retrieval. This archive is unique for its breadth of coverage and currently holds some 600,000 items dating from 1780 to the present day. The collection is international in scope, although there is a strong emphasis on UK and especially London programmes (the hand-list of venues lists 1064 venues in London alone). Runs of programmes are generally stored by location (titles of some of the main runs are given in Appendix 1). Special collections include the archive of the concert agent Ibbs & Tillett, with albums of programmes covering the firm's artists and promotions from the beginning of the twentieth century, and the Arthur Jacobs collection. The Department also receives copies of concert programmes from the Wigmore Hall and London venues. Several valuable finding aids are available (uniquely, for such a major collection in the UK), including card indices of artists, first performances, orchestra lists, subscriber lists and iconographical content. An online catalogue is being developed. The Royal College of Music Library, meanwhile, has a set of Sir George Grove's annotated set of the Crystal Palace Saturday Concert programmes, among other interesting items.

Based at Trinity College of Music, the Mander and Mitchenson Theatre Collection comprises about 1500 archive boxes containing playbills, posters, programmes, engravings, cuttings and photographs of the London and regional theatres, from the earliest days of Drury Lane and

Covent Garden to London's most recent productions. There are files on every actor and actress of note in the British Theatre, material related to circus troupes, dance, opera, music hall, dramatists, singers and composers, together with relevant engravings and pictures. The collection is only partly catalogued and there is no online catalogue.

The Norman McCann archive, held by the Royal Academy of Music Museum, includes an extensive collection of programmes dating from the eighteenth and nineteenth centuries. A project begun in October 2002 aims to provide an online catalogue with individual records for each programme in the collection.

Public libraries

Appendix 1 lists sixteen public libraries in the UK that hold collections of concert programmes. Information about fifteen of these institutions has been gathered during the course of the *Cecilia* project, which included one question that gave respondents the opportunity to indicate that they held collections of concert programmes. A surprising outcome of the survey is that so few public libraries have responded positively to this question. At the time of writing, some three hundred libraries and archives had contributed data to the *Cecilia* project, but only fifteen of the public libraries stated that they had programmes in their collections. In some cases this may reflect the fact that programmes are held in the Serials or General Humanities sections of the libraries and not in the Music Library. Thus the list of programmes for Newcastle City Library given in Appendix 1 was compiled in response to the survey carried out in the preparation of the British Union Catalogue of Music Periodicals (BUCOMP), reflecting the fact that programmes are sometimes treated as serial publications and shelved in that section of the library. The Newcastle listing is valuable as it shows that the City Library has collected much material of relevance to the local musical scene in the North East, dating from 1860 to the present day.

Local studies libraries

Local studies libraries are potentially a major source for concert programmes and ephemera of local significance and a full survey of these institutions is required. I have been able to locate eight libraries that hold significant collections of programmes; further information may be obtained from the Local Studies Group of CILIP (http://www.cilip.org.uk/groups/lsg/). The Lamb Collection at the Central Library in Dundee may be typical. The collection contains several thousand concert programmes dating from 1860 to the 1940s. These are sorted into year order and, where applicable, into concert series sequence, but the collection as a whole remains uncatalogued. A few notable programmes have been selected for digitisation as part of a wider programme focusing on the Lamb Collection. These include programmes of recitals given in Dundee by Sarasate, Bottesini, Joachim and Ysaÿe. There are, in addition, programmes for concerts, *conversaziones* and other miscellaneous musical events spread through the collection of general Victoriana, because they were hosted by a particular local club or were part of fundraising festivals or bazaars for volunteer companies or churches.

Archives

The list of collections of programmes held by public archives in Appendix 1 was compiled mainly from web-based sources, such as the A2A database and the Archives Hub. It lists 114 collections of programmes, or collections that include programmes in them, located in 43 city, county and borough archives across the UK. This represents the tip of the iceberg as far as UK archives are concerned, but the range of material found here is striking. Programmes are preserved in the archives of music clubs and societies (Bedford, Blackpool, Irby, Smethwick), choral societies (Bury, Bradford, Carlisle, Hull, Kendal, Stanwix, Tanfield,), orchestras (Ashton-under-Lyne, Birmingham, Hull, Lancaster, London,

Manchester), operatic societies (Godley), parish churches, schools, and family estates (such as the Austen-Leigh family, held at Hampshire Record Office), as well as railway associations (Cumbria) and the archive of the *East Anglian Magazine*, among others.

Given the local focus of many of these archives, there is less likelihood of duplication between their holdings. Much of the material is unique, even if some collections include programmes of lesser music-historical interest (the programmes of school concerts are a case in point). In many cases, single programmes are mentioned within the context of a larger collection and their significance is best comprehended with reference to that context. The concert programmes preserved in the papers of the Alderman H.G. Mason, for example, derive from the archive of the Plymouth Corporation and papers relating to the delegation that visited Novorossisk in the USSR in 1956. Reference to this wider context would be essential in any union catalogue of concert programmes that included this kind of material.

Academic libraries

Appendix 1 draws together information about programmes held by twenty Higher Education institutions in the UK. Many of the descriptions are at collection level and are based upon data submitted to Collection Level Description projects such as the Archives Hub. Collections of programmes are to be found in various sections of university libraries and in other departments on the university campus. At the University of Reading, for example, programmes are held by three different libraries: the main Whiteknights Library, the Music Library, and the Centre for Ephemera Studies.

Once again, the diversity of material assembled by these institutions is demonstrated in Appendix 1. The University of Leeds, for example, has a large number of archives of material collected by officers and soldiers in the First World War, including programmes of concerts held at the Ruhleben Concentration camp. The university also has a collection of 262 opera and concert programmes assembled by Herbert Thompson, music critic of the *Yorkshire Post* from 1886 until 1936. The value of the collection is enhanced by Thompson's diaries, in which he gives timings for all the music he heard at concerts during the same period. An associated collection, containing programmes and press cuttings collected by Ernest Bradbury, continues the coverage of Yorkshire musical life up to the 1980s.[5] Many university collections also have programmes that relate to the activities of their music departments and local music societies, such as the Bangor Musical Club and the Edinburgh Choral Union. From this brief overview, it seems likely that a more thorough survey of university libraries will reveal many more collections of programmes and concert ephemera.

Performance venues and ensembles

A number of the larger venues maintain their own archives. These notably include the Royal Opera House, the Wigmore Hall, the Royal Festival Hall and the Royal Albert Hall. While these collections will fill many gaps identified in library holdings, access to them is inevitably limited. In some cases, duplicate sets of programmes may be more readily available from a library source, but this should not diminish the value of such archives. They are also more likely to collect concert ephemera, such as posters and leaflets, which can offer significant information about ticket prices, advertising methods, promoters, and iconography. A number of significant performance venues are not known to maintain archives, a situation which will inevitably lead to major gaps in coverage in the long term — even if individual ensembles collect programmes relating to their own events. The Barbican Centre in London is a notable example.

The archive of the English National Opera preserves a wide range of documentation relating to the running of the company from 1931 (it was called Sadler's Wells Opera until 1968) to the present day. This includes administrative files, minutes of meetings, reports, press cuttings,

[5]This collected was collated by Susan Bradbury with a grant from the Music Libraries Trust.

photographs, audio-visual material and a small number of plans and costume designs. The archive also has a number of catalogues and guides available to researchers: these include lists of productions and indexes of files. A database is also in progress.

In Ireland, venues such as the National Concert Hall in Dublin and the Wexford Festival Opera may hold collections of programmes, as may performing groups such as Opera Ireland and the RTÉ Performing Groups (including the National Symphony Orchestra).[6] Many UK orchestras maintain their own collections of programmes. The City of Birmingham Symphony Orchestra, for example, has established an archive at the Symphony Centre in Birmingham. The collection includes a near-complete run of programmes of the CBSO's performances since the Second World War, along with programmes of other associated events. It should be noted that some orchestral collections are inaccessible to researchers and are not always comprehensive. In its early days, the London Symphony Orchestra only archived programmes of concerts the orchestra promoted itself and failed to retain programmes when it was hired by outside organisations.[7] Increasingly orchestras are utilising databases that combine administrative and archival functions. The OPAS system, for example, is becoming widely used. This includes the facility for creating an automatic performance history of each work entered into the database, as well as details of instrumentation and finance.

Concert clubs and societies

Many clubs and societies maintain their own private archives of concert programmes. The number of such private collections held in the UK and Ireland is difficult to estimate with any accuracy. *Making Music* (formerly the National Federation of Music Societies) has several hundred members

[6]Roy Stanley, Trinity College Dublin, personal communication.
[7]The orchestra regularly played for Patron's Fund concerts for the Royal College of Music, but did not archive the programmes (however copies are held by the College in its Department of Portraits and Performance History).

which may be contacted directly (address labels are available from the Federation) or via the organisation's magazine *Making Music News*.[8] It is clear that many archives have significant holdings, and sometimes preserve material that relates to the wider musical scene in the local area. I have selected two examples for further comment.

Cockermouth Harmonic Society

The archive of the Cockermouth Harmonic Society holds a copy of most programmes dating back to the Society's foundation in 1867 (about 100 in total). The Society currently does not deposit copies of its programmes anywhere else, primarily because local libraries are not interested in collecting them.[9] A database has been developed in Lotus Approach to document concert details (date, venue, conductor, forces, works performed), with some JPEG images of the programmes themselves.

Rhyl Music Club

Rhyl Music Club was formed in 1947 and continues to present about 12 concerts per season. During the 1950s and 1960s the club organised orchestral concerts at Rhyl Pavilion in collaboration with the Arts Council of Wales. Orchestras ranged from regional ones, such as the RLPO and the Hallé Orchestra, to London-based ones (e.g. the Royal Philharmonic Orchestra), and a larger number from Eastern and Central Europe. Many noted conductors and soloists came with them. In addition, for a reasonable period in the 1980s and 1990s the Welsh Arts Council arranged tours of visiting foreign chamber orchestras that the Club presented at the Town Hall (in all these total about 100).

Rhyl Music Club holds programmes for these concerts in its archive, together with programmes of the Club's own chamber concerts. Many of these concerts were given by artists of international renown as well as by younger, then unknown players, many of whom later became well known. Dame Myra Hess gave the first professional concert in 1947. The Club

---

[8]An introductory article about the Concert Programmes Project appeared in *Making Music News* in April 2002.

[9]Robert Flower, Cockermouth Harmonic Society.

maintains programme cards listing concerts briefly for the full 55 years, and the annual brochures, giving more detailed information, for most years with some missing in the 1960s and 1970s. A number of individual programmes were lost in this middle period, but the Club retains complete sets for about 40 of the 55 seasons.[10] In total the archive holds some 600-700 programmes. The vast majority is not preserved elsewhere.

As we have seen, some archives of music clubs and societies have also been deposited with local and university libraries and archives, but these are likely to be exceptions to the general rule.

Cathedral Libraries and Archives

Places of worship are traditionally a focal point for musical activity in the UK. The presence of a choir or choir school attached to the institution often provides the impetus for concert giving, but concerts take place at smaller church venues throughout the country. The Aldeburgh Festival also traditionally presents events at church venues in and around Aldeburgh – Aldeburgh Parish Church and Blythburgh Church being two notable examples. Local music clubs and societies often use church venues in the absence of any other suitable or purpose-built halls in smaller towns.

It is likely that many churches in the UK maintain archives of material relating to events in the Church calendar, although only larger institutions make them available to the public. Cathedral libraries and archives are a potentially important source of programmes for cathedral concerts. Westminster Abbey, moreover, has a collection of programmes for concerts held at the Abbey and at St. Margaret's Church, Westminster. The programmes are bound up in volumes with service sheets (from 1901, with examples of individual service sheets dating from 1847 onwards), many of which also have a significant musical content. Norwich Cathedral also maintains a collection of

---

[10] I am grateful to Derek Bartley, Concert Organiser, Rhyl Music Club, for this information.

programmes. Further information about Anglican Cathedral libraries and their holdings may be obtained via the Cathedral Libraries and Archives Association, which is actively engaged in resource discovery and digital projects of various kinds.

4. Current Activity

The project to compile a union catalogue of concert programmes can build on a number of initiatives in the last four years that have improved access to library, archive and museum collections in general, and several that have impacted upon the provision of music resources in the electronic environment in particular.

In 1999, the Full Disclosure report assessed the scope of the problems associated with access to collections that were either completely or partially uncatalogued, or where catalogues were not converted to machine-readable formats. The report called for greater co-ordination between libraries, archives and museums at a strategic level, and the retrospective conversion of catalogue records otherwise held in analogue format, and it identified a need to develop collection level descriptions to map holdings nation-wide. Music materials are touched upon in the report as one subject area requiring attention, but uncatalogued concert ephemera is not specifically mentioned.

In the wake of the Full Disclosure report, a number of projects have been established to provide collection level descriptions that cross institutional or sectoral boundaries. Some of these have been rather broad in scope. AIM25, for example, is a major project aiming to provide electronic access to collection level descriptions of the archives of over fifty higher education institutions and learned societies within the greater London area. The Access to Archives database (A2A) provides a gateway to catalogues from nearly two hundred local record offices and libraries, universities, museums and national and specialist institutions in England, and has a facility to allow users to obtain copies of archive documents online.

Other projects have focused on specific subject areas, such as the performing arts (*Backstage*) and women's history (*Genesis*). Special collections of concert programmes have been covered by some of these projects and they have been used to compile the preliminary list given in the appendices. In general, however, concert programmes fall outside the remit of such descriptive projects, especially where they do not form part of a larger archival collection or are placed within a general sequence of books or periodicals. Many important repositories of programmes, such as the archives of music publishers, performance venues and music societies, do not in any case fall within the scope of the majority of these projects. Concert programmes are also beyond the scope of the major project currently underway to provide a collection level 'map' of music resources in the UK. The *Cecilia* project was launched in August 2001 and aims to harvest information about music materials held by libraries, archives, museums, and private collections, and to make the information available through a single online portal. In general, the descriptions are not intended to give anything more than a general overview of individual collections. Although some collections of programmes have been included, a greater emphasis is placed on describing collections of music manuscripts and printed music.

Other music-related projects have been dedicated to performance sets (*Encore!*), printed music (*Ensemble*), music manuscripts (*Répertoire Internationale des Sources Musicales*), and the holdings of music conservatoire libraries (*Music Libraries Online*). A conference organised at the British Library on 26 March 2002 drew together representatives of these projects and other stakeholders to take stock of developments in recent years and to examine the potential for a truly integrated, distributed online resource for music. As a result, work is currently underway to revise and update the *Libraries and Information Plan for Music*, which was originally published in 1993, to develop a framework for future activity.[1] Elsewhere, progress has been made on cataloguing and describing important collections of printed ephemera that include concert programmes, such as the John Johnson collection at the Bodleian Library.

A few projects are also concerned specifically with concert programmes. To illustrate the range of different approaches currently being pursued, I shall describe six projects currently being developed in the UK and internationally.

---

[1]The revised plan is due to be published in July 2003.

The International Index of Musical Performances

This project was established by David Day at Brigham Young University (Utah, USA) in 2001. It differs from most other equivalent projects in that the focus is not primarily on the concert programme as a printed artefact. Rather, the stated goal is to establish an international project for indexing musical performances, based upon a wide range of primary and secondary source materials. These include advertisements, libretti, press reviews and announcements, almanacs, and annotations in performance materials, as well as concert programmes themselves. A database has been developed using MySQL software and with a web interface to allow for remote input of data.

The database has a relational structure with eight main files: personal names, institutional names, works (with sub-tables for genre and roles), performances, bibliography of performance sources, bibliography of authority sources, an online directory of participating institutions and links to collection level descriptions in the IRMA database.[2] The database has the capacity to link to scanned images of original documents and audio or video excerpts of modern performances. It will also enable users to interrogate the database for statistical data, and to generate reports on particular topics, such as chronologies of theatres or concert halls, artist careers, interpretations of a given role, performance-frequency profiles of works, and chronologies of musical organisations.

Following a demonstration of the database at the IAML meeting in Berkeley (August 2002), the IAML Board agreed to establish a Working Group to co-ordinate the project's future development. The Working Group for the Indexing of Musical Performances aims to build a coalition among existing projects and other similar projects currently under development, as well as to map out a plan for the longer term development of the database itself. Linkage with other related IAML projects, such as the Bibliography Commission and the Working Group on the Exchange of Authority Data, will also form part of the agenda. The sharing of authority files is being discussed as a way to ensure consistency

---

[2]The IAML Working Group on the International Register of Music Archives.

between projects within existing international standards.

Concert Life in Nineteenth-Century London Database

This is an inter-university research project, which brings together academic staff in the music departments of Oxford Brookes University (Christina Bashford), the University of Leeds (Rachel Cowgill) and Goldsmiths College, University of London (Simon McVeigh). The project aims to facilitate empirical research into the nature of concert life and the evolution of repertoire in London during the nineteenth century, by documenting concert life using contemporary newspapers, journals and concert programmes.[3] Funding is provided by Oxford Brookes University, the University of Leeds and the Arts and Humanities Research Board.

The first phase of research began in January 1999 and involved a detailed study of London concert life for selected years in the nineteenth century (1815, 1855 and 1895). This approach was modelled upon the concept of 'Slice History' pioneered by a group of Australian social historians. This involves the detailed documentation of one-year slices of history a generation apart to facilitate comparisons between them. By adopting this methodology, the project leaders recognise the immense growth in concert activity in London during the course of the nineteenth century and the sheer abundance of source material available. By narrowing the focus in this way, they were able to demonstrate feasible outcomes in their bid for funding. The second phase of the project, which involves an investigation of concert life in the 1830s and 1870s, began in 2001.

The data is being entered into a web-based, fully relational database, which has been designed by Communicata Ltd. (now Civic Computing) using Oracle 8 software. The database is constructed around two main

---

[3]For a description of the project see: Christina Bashford, 'Introducing the Concert Life in 19th-Century London Database' in *Brio*, vol.36 no.2 (1999), 111-16 and Christina Bashford, Rachel Cowgill and Simon McVeigh, 'The Concert Life in 19th-century London Database', *Nineteenth-century British Music Studies*, vol.2, ed. Jeremy Dibble and Bennett Zon (Aldershot: Ashgate, 2002), 1-12.

elements: source records and interpretative records. This reflects the variety of source material being studied for the project and the fact that different sources sometimes offer conflicting evidence about a particular event. A new source record is compiled for each document, preserving the integrity of the original. For a single event, there may be any number of source records relating to newspaper announcements, programmes, and reviews. Each interpretative record represents a critical collation of the various source records relating to a particular event. Much of the data entered here is placed under authority control, with links to files of concert venues, people and musical works. The project leaders have also devised a system of confidence rating for any link from the interpretative record to the authority files, allowing a degree of uncertainty to be built into the identification of particular works or people, for example.

The project has much in common with the International Index of Musical Performances, both in terms of its focus upon individual events and in its use of diverse source material. Neither project was conceived as an aid to locating concert programmes, although resource discovery is certainly a valuable spin-off.

The Britten-Pears Library Catalogue of Concert Ephemera

The Britten-Pears Library began cataloguing its collection of programmes and concert ephemera early in 2002 using a specially modified MARC template.[4] By choosing to adopt the MARC format, the library plans to make the catalogue available alongside its existing online catalogues and to enable users to search across all the catalogues simultaneously. A test version of the catalogue was made available from the library's website in August 2002, using software designed by Mikromark Webhotel. The collection is being catalogued at item level, but in varying levels of details depending on the nature of the performance.

---

[4]MARC is an acronym for Machine Readable Cataloguing, originally developed by the Library of Congress in the mid-1960s as a convenient way of storing and exchanging bibliographic records.

Programmes relating to performances involving Benjamin Britten and/or Peter Pears are catalogued in the greatest detail, with complete coverage of the works performed and any programme notes they may have written. Other programmes are catalogued in less detail, with added entries being recorded only for works by Britten and by close associates of the composer. Details of the full programme, however, are summarised in diplomatic transcription in a special notes field.[5] The database facilitates searching on any combination of fields, including: title word, author, performer, date and place of performance, first performance, photographer (for images that have been selected for cataloguing), material type (programme, poster, cutting, flyer), concert series, and free text.

The Library has devised a unique way to catalogue programme books for festivals and concert series that encompass multiple events. Making use of a facility to link records in a hierarchical structure offered by Mikromark, they are able to link records at different levels, with a main record to represent the programme book linked to individual records for each event. Records linked in this way are grouped together in the search results. To take an example, in 1977 a special chamber music festival was mounted at Aldeburgh sponsored by Benson & Hedges. A festival programme was printed, with articles on each of the concerts in the series and five more general articles relating to the festival theme. In the main catalogue record, the booklet is entered under the heading of the festival, with a transcription of the title page and added entries for the author and title of each of the general articles, as well as details of the main photograph of Britten included in the booklet. The opening concert of the festival — a recital of solo piano music by Franz Schubert — was given by the Russian pianist Sviatoslav Richter. In the record for this concert, the programme details are listed without added entries for composers or works and the author of the programme note is listed in the contents field. Numbers of the pages on which the concert details are listed in the programme book are given in the physical description.

---

[5]Field 512 in the MARC record.

UNDER THE IMMEDIATE PATRONAGE OF

His Royal Highness the Prince Regent,

PHILHARMONIC SOCIETY.

First Concert, MONDAY, March 8th, 1813.

PART I.

Overture to Anacreon - - - - - *Cherubini.*
Quartetto, two Violins, Viola and Violoncello, Messrs. F. CRAMER, MORALT, SHERRINGTON, and LINDLEY - - - - - - *Mozart.*
Quartetto & Chorus, Nell' orror, Mrs. MORALT, Messrs. HAWES, P. A. CORRI, and KELLNER *Sacchini.*
Serenade, Wind Instruments, Messrs. MAHON, OLIVER, HOLMES, TULLY, and the PETRIDES *Mozart.*
Symphony - - - - - - - - *Beethoven.*

PART II.

Symphony - - - - - - - - *Haydn.*
Chorus, Placido e' il mar, Mrs. MORALT, Miss HUGHES, Messrs. P. A. CORRI, C. SMITH, &c. *Mozart.*
Quintetto, two Violins, Viola, and two Violoncellos, Messrs. SALOMON, CUDMORE, SHERRINGTON, LINDLEY, and C. ASHLEY - - *Boccherini.*
Chaconne, Jomelle, and March - - - *Haydn.*

Leader, Mr. SALOMON.—Piano-Forte, Mr. CLEMENTI.

The Second will take place on Monday next, the 15th March.

Reynell, Printer, 21, Piccadilly, London.

Pl. 2.
Programme for the inaugural concert of the Philharmonic Society, 13 March 1813.
The British Library K.6.d.3. Reproduced by permission of the BL Board.

The Royal Philharmonic Society Concerts Database

The Royal Philharmonic Society database was specially designed by DMT Associates and documents the history of the Society's concerts from 1813 until the 1980s. The database is approximately three-quarters complete, with records relating to some 1200 performances altogether. Work still needs to be done on the period between 1870 and 1900. The project was established primarily for the Society's own use, to enable it to answer queries about the history of the Society and to aid in the writing of programme notes for future performances. The data was drawn mainly from the RPS's own set of concert programmes, although reference is also made to annotated programmes in the Sir George Smart Collection at the British Library (to 1846).

The database includes one record for each work performed at a concert and has fields for composer/arranger/editor, title/uniform title/'performed as' title, artist, location, and date. A comments field allows additional information to be added. The database allows researchers to assess the position that a composer held in the Society's repertory, by analysing the frequency of performances of a particular work and the chronological range in which a composer's work was represented. It also has a browse function that facilitates the display of records in sequence according to the defined search criteria. The database also provides much useful information to assist with the dating of music manuscripts in the RPS archive, especially where sets of parts can be identified with a particular performance. Future plans for the database include adding authority files for names and titles of works, and making the data available via the web.

Other activity

Two other projects that deal with programmes should also be mentioned. They are both private projects, which are being developed by individuals in each case, and demonstrate distinct approaches to the documentation and recording of data from concert programmes. The historian William Weber (California State University at Long Beach) has designed a database for analysing concert data derived from his research into the musical life of eighteenth- and nineteenth-century London. The database is constructed in FileMaker Pro and facilitates a statistical approach to support Weber's studies of repertory, the decline of the 'miscellaneous' concert, the rise of a canon of musical works, and the place of 'modern' music in the musical life of the period. Weber has begun to populate the database with defined sets of data, in order to promote comparisons between attitudes towards programming and the canon at different times.

The Gustav Mahler database is being developed by the musicologist Paul Banks (Royal College of Music). The aim of this project is to document all performances of Mahler's music in his lifetime, drawing on concert programmes, letters, reviews and concert almanacs published in Germany in the late nineteenth century. An important feature of the database is that it allows the original running order of a programme to be maintained and viewed, allowing the user to locate performances of Mahler's works in the context of its position in the programme as a whole. The database structure is nevertheless fully relational (using Access software), with a controlled vocabulary and authority files for names, performance venues, and titles of works. It also allows for the input of graphics files and the development of a web interface.[6]

[6]Other relevant databases include Simon McVeigh's *Calendar of London Concerts 1750-1800, Advertised in the London Daily Press*, Rosamund McGuinness's *Computer Register of Musical Data in London Newspapers, 1660-1800,* and Stephen Lloyd's *Bournemouth Municipal Orchestra Performances of British Music*, 1895-1929.

5. A Collection of Concert Programmes

Background

In part 2 of this report I gave an indication of the great diversity of the collections of concert programmes held by libraries and archives in the UK and Ireland. They range from discrete runs of programmes for a single venue, to programmes of concerts given in schools and parish churches, to a collection relating to the Vellum Binders' Trade Society in the late nineteenth century. Different collections are interesting for a variety of reasons. The collection of 130 programmes from Granville Bantock's estate, for example, is significant from a biographical point of view, as a source to investigate the composer's activities and the reception of his music.[1] The collection also includes a large archive of letters and cuttings, which are also useful in documenting Bantock's life as composer and conductor. Other collections have much to offer researchers seeking to investigate the musical life through the eyes of people who were active in other ways: notable examples include the collections of the Yorkshire music critic Herbert Thompson and the scholar Sir Donald Tovey.[2]

The collection of an individual music lover may also have much to offer. This type of collection would normally reflect personal interests and may encompass disparate local events, private concerts, or concerts attended abroad. It may also include unusual items that are not preserved elsewhere. In this part of the report I shall examine a representative collection that contains a mixed bag of material, much of it from mainstream venues, but also some potentially unique items. I shall describe its content and the significance of individual items within it, as well as explore some of the problems associated with it. In chapter 6 of the report

[1]The collection is held at Worcestershire Record Office.
[2]At the University of Leeds and University of Edinburgh respectively.

we shall consider how to go about describing the collection as a whole.

Content

The collection was assembled by Diana Gordon over the course of about 43 years and was acquired by the British Library in January 1975. It comprises some 220 opera and concert programmes, dating mainly from the period of 1932 to 1974, for performances given at forty venues altogether. It is typical of the type of miscellaneous collection that one might expect to come from a seasoned London concertgoer. The major London venues, including the Royal Opera House, Sadler's Wells Theatre, and the Wigmore Hall, are strongly represented. But the collection also includes programmes from other less established London venues, such as Central Hall, Westminster, the Institute of Contemporary Arts, and the Italian Institute. There are programmes of opera performances, piano recitals, orchestral concerts, song recitals, carol concerts, and many other musical events. The collection also includes programmes of theatrical events, including performances of Racine plays at the Savoy Theatre (in 1960) and Chekhov's *The Cherry Orchard* at Sadler's Wells in 1958. An overview, arranged by venue, is given in Chapter 6.

As a whole the collection gives a broad overview of London musical life during the period. It demonstrates how concerts developed over a period of 40 years, from Sir Thomas Beecham's Sunday orchestral concerts at the Queen's Hall during the 1930s, to the LSO International Series at the Royal Festival Hall in the 1970s. The historical significance of many programmes in the collection is self-evident. The lavish programme book for the Elgar Memorial Concert documents an event given at the Royal Albert Hall on 24 March 1934, a month after the composer's death (see Plate 3). The concert included performances of the slow movement of Elgar's Second Symphony and *The Dream of Gerontius* conducted by Sir Adrian Boult. Included in the programme are essays by H.C. Colles, drawings of Elgar, and the full libretto of the oratorio. Of equal significance are programme books for various events given at the time of the Coronation in 1953. These include the programme for Britten's ill-fated opera *Gloriana*, given at the Royal Opera House as part of a special Coronation Season in June 1953, and the programme for a series of Coronation Concerts at the Royal Festival Hall.

The collection also sheds light on the performance history of forgotten or neglected repertoire. Samuel Coleridge-Taylor's elaborate dramatic cantata *The Song of Hiawatha*, for example, was staged annually by the Royal Choral Society at the Royal Albert Hall from 1924 until 1940 (the work was also performed in 1946).[1] A souvenir programme was printed for the run of performances given between 8 and 20 June 1936, which were due to be conducted by Sir Malcolm Sargent. The copy found in the Diana Gordon collection, however, includes an errata slip for the performance on 16 June indicating that the conductor Muir Matthieson would replace Sargent at the podium. Other major musical events before the war included Beecham's Sibelius Festival at the Queen's Hall in October and November 1938, an important event in the reception of Sibelius's music in the UK. The series included the complete cycle of Sibelius symphonies, spread over six concerts. The title page of the Festival programme is reproduced in Plate 4.[2]

Diana Gordon also collected programmes that relate to several pioneering concert series of unusual or modern repertory. The Morley College Concerts Society Series is represented by programmes for seven concerts given at Central Hall, Westminster, between 1946 and 1951, most of them conducted by Walter Goehr and Michael Tippett, who was Director of Music at the college from 1940.[3] A particular feature of the concerts was the juxtaposition of recent works with performances of

---

[1]Geoffrey Self, *The Hiawatha Man: The Life and Work of Samuel Coleridge-Taylor* (Aldershot: Scolar Press, 1993), 270-271.

[2]See Maurice Parker, *Sir Thomas Beecham, Bart, C.H. (1879-1961): a calendar of his concert and theatrical performances* (Westcliff-on-Sea: Sir Thomas Beecham Society, 1985). Excellent calendar of Beecham's performances, primarily based on newspaper reviews. See also Tony Benson, *Sir Thomas Beecham Bart, CH, 1879-1961: supplement to Maurice Parker's calendar of Sir Thomas's concert and theatrical performances*, Issue 2 (Westcliff-on-Sea: Sir Thomas Beecham Society, 1998), 290.

[3] Ian Kemp, *Tippett: the composer and his music* (London: Eulenburg Books, 1984), 40-47.

X.435/318.

ROYAL ALBERT HALL

The Royal Choral Society

WITH THE CO-OPERATION OF THE

British Broadcasting Corporation

Elgar Memorial Concert

SATURDAY AFTERNOON
MARCH 24th, 1934
at 2.30 p.m.

Under the Patronage of Their Majesties The King and Queen

THE DREAM OF GERONTIUS

ASTRA DESMOND
STEUART WILSON ROY HENDERSON

The B.B.C. Symphony Orchestra
Leader: ARTHUR CATTERALL
and
The London Philharmonic Orchestra
Leader: PAUL BEARD

Conductors:
ADRIAN BOULT AND SIR LANDON RONALD
At the Organ: R. ARNOLD GREIR

The Profits of this Concert will go to the MUSICIANS' BENEVOLENT FUND, of which Society the late SIR EDWARD ELGAR was President.

Pl. 3.
Programme for the Elgar Memorial Concert, Royal Albert Hall, 24 March 1934.
The British Library X.435/318. Reproduced by permission of the BL Board.

English music of sixteenth and seventeenth centuries, such as Tallis's forty-part motet *Spem in Alium* (on 21 November 1947 and 5 March 1948) and Purcell's *Ode on St. Cecilia's Day* of 1692 (also on 21 November 1947). The 1948 series also featured the first London performance of Monteverdi's *L'Incoronazione di Poppea*, conducted by Walter Goehr on 21 May of that year. Tippett's preoccupation with the music of Purcell, Tallis and their contemporaries found its expression in his own music immediately after the war, as he sought to forge a distinctively English musical language by adopting techniques from the past.[4] Tippett himself contributed programme notes for some of the concerts and they give some insight into his thinking at this time. His note on Purcell's *Ode* is characteristic:

> In my opinion the only composer who can be compared with Purcell for impeccable musical sense of the English language is Dowland. Purcell's musical apparatus is much more complicated than Dowland's. But, however complicated it becomes, the secret of its interpretation, at least in all the music with voices, remains the language. If the language is sung in all voices with poetic understanding as well as due regard to the musical style of the time and place, then the wonderful polyphony sounds clear in all its beauty. Though I have known and worked with the score of this Ode for many years, there are still details of interest which surprise me in that I had not noticed them before. I doubt if Bach even is a greater contrapuntist than Purcell. But the Ode on St. Cecilia's Day is not only detail, it is also measure and balance in the great design of this lengthy work. It is spacious and serene. It is an English masterpiece.

Two series of concerts at the Wigmore Hall were prominent during the 1940s. The Edward Clark Series paid particular attention to the music of

---

[4]The slow movement of his first symphony, for example, adopts ground bass principles drawn from Purcell. See David Clarke, 'Michael Tippett', *The New Grove Dictionary of Music Online* ed. L. Macy (Accessed 16 October 2002), http://www.grovemusic.com. See also: Michael Tippett, 'Our Sense of Continuity in English Drama and Music', *Henry Purcell, 1659-1695: Essays on his Music*, ed. I. Holst (London: Oxford University Press, 1959), 42-51.

Six Concerts

OF THE WORKS OF

JEAN SIBELIUS

WILL BE GIVEN AT

QUEEN'S HALL

Sole Lessees - - - - CHAPPELL & Co., Ltd.

OCTOBER	27TH	. .	8.15 p.m.
NOVEMBER	1ST	. .	8.15 p.m.
NOVEMBER	5TH	. .	3 p.m.
NOVEMBER	11TH		8.15 p.m.

AND AT

ÆOLIAN HALL

NEW BOND STREET, W.1

OCTOBER	29TH	. .	3 p.m.
NOVEMBER	12TH	. .	8.15 p.m.

THE

LONDON PHILHARMONIC ORCHESTRA

Under the Direction of

SIR THOMAS BEECHAM, Bart.

Pl. 4.
Sibelius Festival Programme, Queen's Hall, October and November 1938.
The British Library X.435/318. Reproduced by permission of the BL Board.

the Second Viennese School, with a heady mixture of music by major contemporary composers of other European countries. The concert on 18 January 1946, for example, included music by Prokofiev, Berg, Lambert, Lutyens, and Milhaud. For the front cover of the programmes the organisers commissioned a special illustration from the artist Michael Ayrton (see Plate 5).[5] The Boosey & Hawkes Concert Series also presented challenging new repertory: the concert on 27 March 1943 included first performances of Bernard Stevens's Piano Trio and Tippett's Second String Quartet. Later, the Macnaghten Concerts featured music by contemporary British composers and a number of first performances. The Alan Rawsthorne Memorial Concert on 24 November 1971 presented the posthumous premiere of his *Theme and Four Studies* for piano, performed by John Ogdon. The programme booklet includes tributes from William Walton, Alun Hoddinott, Gerard Schurman, and Gordon Green, as well as a catalogue of Rawsthorne's works and a selection of photographs of the composer.

Other notable first performances documented in the Diana Gordon collection include the London premiere of Britten's *War Requiem* (Westminster Abbey on 6 December 1962), the world premiere of Robert Simpson's Symphony no.5 (Royal Festival Hall on 3 May 1973), the first UK stage performance of Berg's *Lulu* (given by the Hamburg State Opera in October 1962), and the English stage premiere of Haydn's opera *Il mondo della Luna*, performed by Philomusica of London at the St. Pancras Arts Festival in 1960.

Performances by major artists are also represented in the collection. In November 1959, for example, Igor Stravinsky and Jean Cocteau collaborated on a performance of *Oedipus Rex* at the Royal Festival Hall

---

[5]Edward Clark was programme builder for the BBC until 1936 and a champion of contemporary music. He served as secretary and president of the ISCM between 1936 and 1952 and was chairman of the London Contemporary Music Centre from 1947 until 1952. See Jennifer Doctor, 'Edward Clark', *The New Grove Dictionary of Music Online* ed. L. Macy (Accessed 23 October 2002), http://www.grovemusic.com.

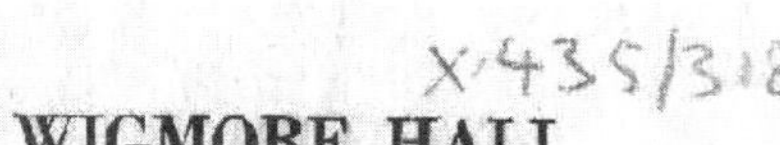

WIGMORE HALL

Wigmore Street, W.1

Second

EDWARD CLARK CONCERT

Friday, 18th January, 1946

at 6.45

Ibbs & Tillett
124 Wigmore Street, W.1

PROGRAMME 6d.

Pl. 5.

Programme for the second Edward Clark Concert, Wigmore Hall, 18 January 1946.
The British Library X.435/318. Reproduced by permission of the BL Board.

on the invitation of the BBC (see Plate 6). Cocteau – who was also librettist of the work – took the part of the speaker in a performance that was later recorded for broadcast on the Third Programme. The programme includes the libretto and programme notes by David Drew. Many of the opera programmes also document performances by great artists of the post-war generation. To mention only one, the legendary Covent Garden performances of Bellini's *Norma* in November 1952 featured Maria Callas in the title role and Joan Sutherland as Clothilde. The conductor was Vittorio Gui.

Many collections of programmes contain miscellaneous items of concert ephemera associated with the events, such as flyers, tickets, and subscription information, and the Diana Gordon Collection is no exception. Three examples will suffice to give an indication of the variety of material that may be preserved. One of the operatic highlights of the 1970s was the performance of Wagner's *Ring* conducted by Reginald Goodall at the London Coliseum. A flyer announcing the complete cycles planned for 1973 includes details of the casts, dates of performances, prices and subscription information – details that may be difficult to obtain elsewhere. Also preserved in the collection is the complete libretto of Stravinsky's *The Rake's Progress*, published by Boosey & Hawkes in 1951. Libretti are commonly sold or distributed at performances of operatic or vocal works, so it is not surprising to find this item in the collection, although there is no accompanying programme. More unusual is an analysis of Roger Smalley's *Missa Parodia I and II*, which was provided as an insert to the programme of a Macnaghten concert given at the Wigmore Hall on 6 October 1967.

As we have seen, programme notes can often yield significant information and many programmes in the Diana Gordon collection include essays by composers or noted scholars. The programme for Artur Schnabel's recital at the Cambridge Theatre in London in 1939 includes an

ROYAL FESTIVAL HALL

(General Manager: T. E. Bean, C.B.E.)

Monday 9 *November* 1959 *at* 11 *p.m.*

BBC Third Programme presents

ŒDIPUS REX

STRAVINSKY

(*Born* 1882)

An Opera-Oratorio after Sophocles.
Text by Jean Cocteau, translated into Latin by J. Daniélou

Œdipus	HELMUT MELCHERT
Jocasta	IRMA KOLASSI
Créon	THOMAS HEMSLEY
Tirésias	MICHAEL LANGDON
The Shepherd	DUNCAN ROBERTSON
The Messenger	ROGER STALMAN
The Speaker	JEAN COCTEAU

THE BBC MEN'S CHORUS

(Chorus Master: Leslie Woodgate)

THE BBC SYMPHONY ORCHESTRA

(Leader: Paul Beard)

Conductor

IGOR STRAVINSKY

A performance of Œdipus Rex *with tonight's orchestra, chorus and soloists under Igor Stravinsky will be broadcast in the Third Programme on Saturday,* 12 *December at* 8.55 *p.m.*

In accordance with the requirements of the London County Council

I. The public may leave at the end of the performance or exhibition by all exit doors, and such doors must at that time be open.

II. All gangways, corridors, staircases and external passageways intended for exit shall be kept entirely free from obstruction, whether permanent or temporary.

III. Persons shall not be permitted to stand or sit in any of the gangways intersecting the seating or to sit in any of the other gangways.

SMOKING IS NOT PERMITTED IN THE AUDITORIUM

Pl. 6.
Programme for Stravinsky's *Oedipus Rex*, Royal Festival Hall, 9 November 1959
The British Library X.435/318. Reproduced by permission of the BL Board.

essay by William Glock on Schubert's late piano music. Other notable examples include Mosco Carner's essay on Mozart's chamber music, for a concert given at the Cambridge Theatre on 13 February 1938, and Denis Arnold on Monteverdi's *Vespers*, for a performance by the Monteverdi Choir and John Eliot Gardiner on 30 September 1967.

As a whole, the Diana Gordon Collection contains much useful and interesting material that fills a number of gaps in the British Library's collections. Of the forty venues represented in the collection, the library holds programmes for only nine of them at different pressmarks. However, the gaps in the coverage of even important venues are considerable. The library's main collection of Royal Festival Hall programmes begins only at 1957, missing out the first six years of the Hall's existence. Of the twenty Festival Hall programmes in the Diana Gordon Collection, eleven of them date from between 1951 and 1957, which goes a small way towards filling this surprising lacuna. Similarly, the Library does not have a separate run of programmes for performances at the Wigmore Hall or the Royal Opera House, so any exemplars from these venues add to the Library's holdings (it should be noted, of course, that both institutions maintain archives of concert programmes and related material). On the other hand, a few items duplicate programmes that the Library already has: for example, copies of two programmes in the 1936–37 season of Beecham Sunday Concerts, given on 31 January and 21 March 1937, are also found at two other locations in the Library.[6]

Problems

Arrangement

We have seen that the vast majority of programmes in the Diana Gordon Collection are not held elsewhere in the British Library, even though the Library does hold programmes from various venues represented in the Collection, such as the Royal Festival Hall. From an organisational point of view, it may make sense to merge collections items together, to form a

---

[6]At pressmarks P.431/290 and d.479.

more complete sequence of programmes at a single location in the library, rather than placing related material at different pressmarks. The major advantage of taking this approach is the improved access to the material that would flow from treating it as a single entity. There are equally good reasons for not splitting up material in a collection in this way, but to maintain its status as a single entity that reflects the tastes and activities of a particular collector. Without reference to the collection's wider context, for example, it would be impossible to understand many of the manuscript annotations that appear in several of the programmes.

The Diana Gordon Collection could be organised in several different ways, although there are no simple solutions to the problem of matching different sizes and formats with a coherent sequence by venue or chronology. The collection is currently divided into eight envelopes roughly according to size and date. The formats range from bound programmes with glossy colour photos, to single typed sheets and flyers. The collection could be reordered to create separate volumes of programmes for venues that are particularly well represented, such as the Royal Opera House and the Sadler's Wells Theatre. In these cases, the programmes tend to be similar in format and size, since they were normally designed by the venue itself for performances by resident companies. Other venues, such as the Wigmore Hall, are more likely to host performances by a range of different groups and ensembles and may have little or no input in the design of their programmes. There may be no consistency in the way in which programmes were presented, making it more difficult to arrange them in clear and consistent chronological sequences.

Last minute changes

Like any other type of source material, a concert programme should not be accepted uncritically as the authoritative account of an event. It is a fact of life that changes of artist or repertory can be forced upon an organiser at the last minute for any number of reasons, or a concert can be cancelled or postponed. Programmes should always be read in conjunction with other related sources, such as newspaper reviews or advertisements, to verify specific details. Brochures of concert series should be approached with extra caution, since they are often compiled some time in advance of the opening concert, making it more likely that the programme would be out-of-date before the series actually started. A good illustration of this is the brochure for Sir Thomas Beecham's Sibelius Festival in London in October and November 1938. As well as programmes for each separate event, the organisers printed a special festival brochure with details of the whole series, which was clearly produced some time in advance of the first concert and does not take into account last-minute changes to the programmes.

The afternoon concert on 29 October was to have featured the Finnish soprano Aulikki Rautawaara as the soloist in Sibelius's *Rakastava*, but according to a newspaper review of the concert she was unable to appear, apparently because of a delayed flight. In place of *Rakastava*, Beecham conducted pieces from Sibelius's *King Christian Suite*, op.27, and the *Scènes Historiques*, op.25. Later that evening Beecham received a telegram from Sibelius (who had apparently heard the concert on the radio) expressing his 'admiration and heartfelt thanks for [the] glorious performance'.[7] There are doubtless many more similar illustrations of the dangers of accepting programmes at face value.[8] It should also be noted that annotated copies of programmes, or erratum slips, can give information about last-minute changes that may not be documented elsewhere (as in the example of Coleridge-Taylor's *Hiawatha* mentioned above).

Problems of identification

Programmes that give relatively few details of the venue, performers, or date of the performance pose a particularly thorny problem to the cataloguer. Of the 220 programmes in the Diana Gordon Collection, three do not give any indication of the performance venue. One of these examples is particularly difficult to deal with, but is also quite typical of

---

[7]Benson, *Sir Thomas Beecham Bart, CH, 1879-1961: supplement to Maurice Parker's calendar of Sir Thomas's concert and theatrical performances*, p.290.

[8]For other examples see Stephen Lloyd, 'Ephemera of concert life: programmes and press cuttings', in Information Sources in Music, ed. Lewis Foreman (Munich: K.G. Saur, 2003), 348-51.

the kinds of problems that arise with programmes of informal or private concerts. The concert in question included a selection of chamber works by Daniel Jones, Roberto Gerhard and Paul Hindemith. The programme was typed on a single sheet and it is undated. There is also no information about the venue or names of performers, but there are brief notes on each of the works that may give a clue to the date of the performance. The most recent piece on the programme was Gerhard's *Three Impromptus* for piano of 1950. The composer wrote the notes for this piece himself, describing it as embodying a changing approach to serial technique:

> The idea underlying the new approach was the wish to divest the series entirely of thematic significance or 'obligations' and to retain its pure combination-value as an instrument of composition. The series will therefore never act as a 'motivo' in the Schoenbergian sense. The new approach presupposes a change of point of view with regard to the series itself: it is no longer considered as a sequence of pitches or, if you like, as a line, but as one single twelve-note structure, or as smaller and larger groups, each group being always regarded as a primary entity.

Gerhard elaborates on the same subject in a 1956 article in *The Score* and this development of the serial technique is reflected in much of his work during the early 1950s.[9] This internal evidence suggests that the concert must have taken place after 1950, and probably took place some time in the 1950s, but it is not immediately possible to establish a firm date or to identify the performers or venue. Other pieces of evidence, including an advertisement in the issue of *The Score* for March 1955, indicate that the performance probably took place at the Wigmore Hall on 13 June 1955.[10]

---

[9]See also Roberto Gerhard, 'Developments in 12-Tone Technique', *The Score*, no.17 (1956), 61-72.

[10]I am grateful to Oliver Davies for locating this advertisement. Both the advertisement and a flyer (preserved in the RCM Department of Portraits and Performance History) for the concert on 13 June 1955, list Daniel Jones's String Quartet no.8 and Hindemith's String Quartet no.4, the other two works that appear on the programme in the Diana Gordon

This is typical of the cataloguing problems that can be encountered with concert programmes. In some cases, and especially with programmes of the eighteenth and nineteenth centuries, the identities of the works performed are also difficult to establish. Generic titles, such as 'symphony' or 'sonata', are frequently impossible to pin down (see the programme of the inaugural concert of the Philharmonic Society, reproduced in Plate 2).

Collection. The fourth advertised work—Dallapiccola's *Quaderno musicale di Annalibera* for piano (1952)—is not listed on the programme.

6. Collection Level Description

Given the large numbers of uncatalogued collections of programmes identified in this report, and the expectation that many more collections remain to be discovered, the potential scope of a union catalogue with records at item level is clearly immense. There are, however, good practical reasons for taking a two-stage approach, and for starting at a higher level of disclosure. The most pressing current need is for a simple mapping of UK and Ireland collections, to enable users to locate the material relating to a particular venue, orchestra, institution, or collector – a directory of descriptions of collections, rather than a catalogue of programmes as such. This would also provide the framework for the second stage of the project, at which point programmes would be catalogued individually.

In this chapter, we shall briefly examine two potential models for describing collections at the higher collection level. The first is similar to the structure adopted for the *British Union Catalogue of Music Periodicals* (*BUCOMP*), which was first published in 1985 and reissued in an updated edition in 1998. A directory along these lines would be suitable for delivery in print format. The second model would build on the work already carried out on the *Cecilia* project and would aim to deliver an online database of collection descriptions, possibly with direct hyperlinks to holding institutions and/or to corresponding *Cecilia* records.

The *BUCOMP* model

In the *British Union Catalogue of Music Periodicals* (*BUCOMP*) serial music publications are listed by title, with details of holding institutions.[1] This model works extremely well for discrete runs of programmes held by a single institution. The list of programmes held by Newcastle City Library in Appendix 1 was compiled from the library's return to the *BUCOMP* project and gives a complete summary of the library's holdings, with an indication of the chronological limits of each collection. The entries may be further organised into one sequence by location, then alphabetically by venue or title of the series. Each holding institution would be given, with an indication of the scope of their holdings, thus:

NEWCASTLE
Newcastle Harmonic Society
Newcastle City Library (1892–1912)

This type of listing obviously leaves a number of questions unanswered. Is the collection of programmes of the *Newcastle Harmonic Society* complete, or are there gaps? When was the Society established and when did it finish? How many programmes does the collection hold altogether? How many concerts were there per year? Where in Newcastle did the Society mount its performances? What information do the programmes contain? Are there lists of performers, works, programme notes? Are the programmes bound in a volume, or loose? Finding answers to these questions would substantially broaden the scope of the project and would require a significant descriptive element to be included in the directory, which may become too unwieldy for publishing in book format. The essential elements of a description should be chosen to fit a model that would be realistic, practical, and offer demonstrable results.

It should also be flexible enough to cope with varying types of collections, reflecting the multiplicity of contexts in which programmes are found. This is especially true in the case of miscellaneous collections of programmes, of which the Diana Gordon Collection is a good example. The following two pages give an example of how the collection can be described at the most basic level and in a format that fits the *BUCOMP* model. To compile this description from scratch required a considerable investment of time, given that a hand-list of the collection was not available and the collection itself is not sorted in coherent way. The resulting description gives a clear and comprehensive overview, even if it gives no indication of the collection's arrangement and cannot be used as an aid for locating individual items. A problem arises with programmes that do not give the location at which the concert took place, placed here under the heading 'unknown'. Without giving details of the works that were performed, the date, or the names of performers or ensembles, it will be impossible to match these programmes with exemplars held by other institutions. For the user, it is hardly useful to know that the collection contains programmes for three concerts that took place at unknown venues. Thus a useful addition to the directory would be brief descriptions of such miscellaneous collections, giving general information about accessibility, provenance, general content and the availability of hand-lists.

Programmes in the Diana Gordon Collection by location and venue

BERLIN
Berliner Ensemble am Schiffbauerdamm
Lbl, Diana Gordon Collection (1 programme)

LIVERPOOL
Royal Court Theatre
Lbl, Diana Gordon Collection (1956; 1 programme)

LONDON
A.D.C. Theatre
Lbl, Diana Gordon Collection (1954; 1 programme)

Aldwych Theatre
Lbl, Diana Gordon Collection (1956–67; 6 programmes)

Cambridge Theatre
Lbl, Diana Gordon Collection (1937–39; 5 programmes)

Caxton Hall, Westminster
Lbl, Diana Gordon Collection (1948; 1 programme)

Central Hall, Westminster
Lbl, Diana Gordon Collection (1946–51; 8 programmes)

Chelsea Town Hall
Lbl, Diana Gordon Collection (1948; 1 programme)

Church of the Holy Sepulchre, Holborn
Lbl, Diana Gordon Collection (1969; 1 programme)

Conway Hall
Lbl, Diana Gordon Collection (1967; 1 programme)

Guildhall School of Music and Drama
Lbl, Diana Gordon Collection (1949-63; 2 programmes)

Hendon Grammar School
Lbl, Diana Gordon Collection (1956; 1 programme)

Institute of Contemporary Arts
Lbl, Diana Gordon Collection (1 programme)

The Italian Institute
Lbl, Diana Gordon Collection (1953-54; 6 programmes)

London Coliseum
Lbl, Diana Gordon Collection (1973; 2 programmes)

Palace Theatre
Lbl, Diana Gordon Collection (3 programmes)

Priory Church of St. Bartholomew-the-Great
Lbl, Diana Gordon Collection (1955; 1 programme)

Purcell Room
Lbl, Diana Gordon Collection (1973; 1 programme)

Queen Elizabeth Hall
Lbl, Diana Gordon Collection (3 programmes)

Queen's Hall
Lbl, Diana Gordon Collection (1935-39; 7 programmes)

Royal Albert Hall
Lbl, Diana Gordon Collection (1932-50; 8 programmes)

Royal Court Theatre
Lbl, Diana Gordon Collection (1965; 1 programme)

Royal Festival Hall
Lbl, Diana Gordon Collection (1951-74; 20 programmes)

Royal Opera House, Covent Garden
Lbl, Diana Gordon Collection (1937-62; 17 programmes)

Sadler's Wells Theatre
Lbl, Diana Gordon Collection (1953-67; 33 programmes)

Savoy Theatre
Lbl, Diana Gordon Collection (1960-62; 3 programmes)

St. James's Church, Piccadilly
Lbl, Diana Gordon Collection (1 programme)

St. John's Lutheran Church, Gresham Street
Lbl, Diana Gordon Collection (1972; 1 programme)

St. John's Smith Square
Lbl, Diana Gordon Collection (1 programme)

St. Martin-in-the-Fields
Lbl, Diana Gordon Collection (1948-69; 3 programmes)

St. Pancras Arts Festival
Lbl, Diana Gordon Collection (1960; 1 programme)

Stoll Theatre
Lbl, Diana Gordon Collection (1 programme)

Theatre Royal, Drury Lane
Lbl, Diana Gordon Collection (1963; 2 programmes)

Victoria and Albert Museum
Lbl, Diana Gordon Collection (1966; 1 programme)

Westminster Abbey
Lbl, Diana Gordon Collection (1939, 1962; 2 programmes)

Wigmore Hall
Lbl, Diana Gordon Collection (1943-72; 16 programmes)

Auditorium, John Lewis (London)
Lbl, Diana Gordon Collection (1965; 1 programme)

MADRID
Teatro de la Zarzuela, Madrid
Lbl, Diana Gordon Collection (1 programme)

OXFORD
Sheldonian Theatre, Oxford
Lbl, Diana Gordon Collection (1965; 1 programme)

UNKNOWN
Lbl, Diana Gordon Collection (2 programmes)

The CLD metadata schema

The Collection Level Description (CLD) metadata schema was developed by UKOLN[1] as part of the Research Support Libraries Programme (RSLP) and is the standard by which a number of RSLP-funded projects, including *Cecilia*, have been developed in recent years. The aim of the schema is to 'devise mapping conventions which enable scholars to read the map of the landscape fruitfully, at the appropriate level of generality or specificity.'[2] It is particularly useful for describing archival collections where contextual information is required to understand the content or provenance of the collection, or its relationship with other collections. The framework prescribes three main elements relating to the collection itself:

- descriptive attributes about the collection
- descriptive attributes about the location (or locations)
- identification of other collections that are related to the collection being described

The framework also requires the identification and/or description of three related agents: the collector; the owner of the collection; and the administrator of the location. This model therefore allows for the documentation of substantially more information than would be possible in a printed directory. Separate authority files for locations and names (personal and corporate, such as the names of venues) would make it possible to link records in a hierarchical structure, or to clarify relationships between them. The main elements required for describing collections of concert programmes would include:

- holding institution record, including details of address, opening times, etc.
- title of collection or concert series, etc.
- names of venues, ensembles, institutions, and associated people
- descriptive overview of content
- accrual status (i.e. is the collection being added to?)

The holding institution record in this instance could be drawn from *Cecilia*, or alternatively a link could be established with *Cecilia* to minimise duplication of material and to maximise efficiency (it is to be expected that some new location records will have to be compiled as the project unearths collections in new locations). The technical solution for the project should use the RSLP collection description schema as its basis and would enable hyperlinks to location records in *Cecilia* and to institutional websites. A web-interface would need to include 'search' and 'browse' functions and allow searching for location, personal name, venue, and free text. The following example gives a draft description of the Diana Gordon Collection and explains the various elements that may be required for describing collections of concert programmes.

Collection Level Description

Collection Attributes

Title

A collection of English ballet, concert, opera and theatre programmes and similar material.

Description

The collection consists of some 220 opera and concert programmes, dating mainly from the period of 1932 to 1974, for performances given at forty venues altogether. The collection was assembled by Diana Gordon and donated to the British Library in 1975. Consists mainly of programmes of the major London venues, including the Royal Opera House, the Sadler's Wells Theatre, the Royal Festival Hall, and the Wigmore Hall.

Strengths

Mainly London venues

Languages

English, Spanish, German

Access restrictions

None

Accrual Status

Closed

Collection Level Description

Name (personal or corporate name associated with the items in the collection)

Diana Gordon

British Library

Berliner Ensemble am Schiffbauerdamm (1 programme)

Royal Court Theatre (1956; 1 programme)

A.D.C. Theatre (1954; 1 programme)

Aldwych Theatre (1956-67; 6 programmes)

Cambridge Theatre (1937-39; 5 programmes)

Caxton Hall, Westminster (1948; 1 programme)

Central Hall, Westminster (1946-51; 8 programmes)

Chelsea Town Hall (1948; 1 programme)

Church of the Holy Sepulchre, Holborn (1969; 1 programme)

Conway Hall (1967; 1 programme)

Guildhall School of Music and Drama (1949-63; 2 programmes)

Hendon Grammar School (1956; 1 programme)

Institute of Contemporary Arts (1 programme)

The Italian Institute (1953-54; 6 programmes)

London Coliseum (1973; 2 programmes)

Palace Theatre (3 programmes)

Priory Church of St. Bartholomew-the-Great (1955; 1 programme)

Purcell Room (1973; 1 programme)

Queen Elizabeth Hall (3 programmes)

Queen's Hall (1935-39; 7 programmes)

Royal Albert Hall (1932-50; 8 programmes)

Royal Court Theatre (1965; 1 programme)

Royal Festival Hall (1951-74; 20 programmes)

Royal Opera House, Covent Garden (1937-62; 17 programmes)

Sadler's Wells Theatre (1953-67; 33 programmes)

Savoy Theatre (1960-62; 3 programmes)

St. James's Church, Piccadilly (1 programme)

St. John's Lutheran Church, Gresham Street (1972; 1 programme)

St. John's Smith Square (1 programme)

St. Martin-in-the-Fields (1948-69; 3 programmes)

St. Pancras Arts Festival (1960; 1 programme)

Stoll Theatre (1 programme)

Theatre Royal, Drury Lane (1963; 2 programmes)

Victoria & Albert Museum (1966; 1 programme)

Westminster Abbey (1939, 1962; 2 programmes)

Wigmore Hall (1943-72; 16 programmes)

Auditorium, John Lewis, London (1965; 1 programme)

Teatro de la Zarzuela, Madrid (1 programme)

Sheldonian Theatre, Oxford (1965; 1 programme)

Collection Level Description

Place (spatial coverage of items in the collection)
Berlin
Liverpool
London
Oxford
Madrid

Time (temporal coverage of items in the collection)
1932-74

Dates
Accumulation date range
1932-74
Contents date range (the range of dates of the individual items within the collection)
1932-74

Associated agents
Collector: Diana Gordon

Owner
The British Library

External relationships
Sub-collection (name of a second collection contained within the current collection)
N/A

Super-collection (name of a second collection that contains the current collection)
N/A

Catalogue or description
N/A

Described collection (name of a second collection described by the current collection)
N/A

Associated collection (name of a second collection associated by provenance)
N/A

Associated publication
Rupert Ridgewell, *Concert Programmes in the UK and Ireland: A Preliminary Report* (London: IAML (UK & Irl) and MLT, 2003)

Reference
BL X.435/318

Dates of creation
1932-1974

Name of creator
Diana Gordon

Extent
220 programmes

Administrative/Biographical History
Unknown

Scope and Content
System of Arrangement
Eight envelopes, arranged according to size and date of performance

Access conditions
None

Immediate Source of Acquisition
Donated in 1975

Finding Aids
Hand-list available

Practical considerations

The preliminary list of collections given in this report clearly only touches the surface of the total resource in the UK and Ireland, although it will form a useful basis for further research. Locating other collections will be a major package of work for the project especially in its early stages, and there are several avenues of enquiry available to reach potential contributors. *Making Music*, for example, provides a mailing list and a regular magazine for its members, which can be used to reach music clubs and societies in the UK. There are also electronic mailing lists for local studies librarians and for orchestral librarians, two groups that are barely represented in the preliminary list of collections, but which may be expected to make a significant contribution. Private archives are altogether more difficult to reach and their identification will necessarily rely to some extent on the collaboration of researchers working in the field.

The collection of data will rely to a great extent on the willingness of contributors to spend time providing descriptions via electronic or paper questionnaires. In many cases this will involve checking the shelves, or drawing up a hand-list, to find out exactly where the 'gaps' in a collection are and what it contains. For some major repositories of programmes, this process will be beyond the resources of the institution itself and it will be necessary to support the process directly by providing funding or practical assistance. The estimated funding requirement for the project will need to address the staffing and training costs that this activity will demand. The benefits of a comprehensive description must also be balanced against the limits of time and resources. To take one notable example, the British Library's collection of Royal Festival Hall programmes covers the period from October 1957 to the present day. There are considerable gaps in the coverage, but it nevertheless consists of no fewer than six hundred large envelopes containing as many as forty programmes each. To describe this collection at an ideal level of detail, and to identify all the gaps in it, will require a substantial input in terms of time and resources. It may, however, be worthwhile to focus initially on the larger collections, such as those preserved by the British Library and the Royal College of Music, to build a critical mass of data before targeting other repositories. Where possible the process of description should also be tied in with a programme of binding and conservation. By making collections more 'visible', a likely knock-on effect of the project will be an increase in user demand, with obvious implications in terms of collection security and conservation. No useful generalisations can be made here since different collections will have different needs, but this element may also have to be considered for project funding.

The precise costing will depend to some extent upon the parameters set down by the funding body applied to, but it is useful to make a comparison with related projects, notably *Cecilia* and *Backstage*. *Cecilia* was granted £51,000 from the British Library Co-operation and Partnership Programme for a 15-month project in two stages. The aim was to harvest records from 250 institutions in the UK. The main cost elements were: salaries for one full-time project officer for the duration of the project, a project assistant for nine months; fees to a consultant charged with designing a technical solution; funding for computer equipment, survey materials, server space, software, and publicity. The concert programmes project may be expected to cover a similar number of institutions, but it would also involve substantially more records (many institutions have multiple collections of programmes) at a slightly higher level of detail. Funding should therefore be sought for a minimum of two years in the first instance. The staffing model should also reflect the amount of extra work involved in creating descriptions for larger collections of programmes and should include one project manager plus three assistants for the duration of the project. Another cost element will be the design of the database and web interface, to facilitate the remote input of data and access to the database upon completion. The total cost may therefore amount to at least twice the funding secured for *Cecilia*.

7. Towards a Union Catalogue

Scope

A full union catalogue of concert programmes in the UK and Ireland, with records at item level (i.e. a record for each individual programme), would undoubtedly bring major benefits in terms of access and collection development. Most importantly it would 'unlock' a resource that is virtually inaccessible to researchers, making it possible to search for programmes relating to particular artists, composers, or ensembles for the first time. The scope of such a project is clearly immense, although it is impossible at this stage to estimate with any accuracy the total number of programmes involved. The three major London collections – the British Library, the Royal College of Music and the Royal Academy of Music – alone hold considerably more than one million programmes and a catalogue of these collections would in itself be extremely valuable. The successful completion of a collection-level 'map' will help to define the scope of the project by giving a much more detailed picture of the degree of duplication between collections. This will, in turn, make it possible to identify priorities and to develop a practical and financial model for the project.

It will almost certainly be necessary to take a staged approach, depending on the amount of funding available, by limiting the initial scope of the project by focusing on a relatively small number of representative collections, or to concentrate on a particular period or location. The datasets model adopted by the Concert Life in Nineteenth-Century London Database project is a good example of this approach. Ideally concert programmes should be catalogued with a similar degree of care and attention to detail as sheet music or printed books. As we have seen, programmes often include information of primary importance, such as programme notes and illustrations, and are witnesses to musical events. Unlike many books, however, concert programmes are not normally identified as the work of a single author or editor and may include essays by a number of writers. The title element is also different, in that it is normally descriptive of a musical event and not of the programme book itself. In many cases there is no title at all. To describe a programme, therefore, it is necessary to give such details as the venue and date of performance, the names of performers and the details of works being performed, including titles and names of composers. This level of description may not be problematic with a solo piano recital, with one performer and only a few works, but what about an opera performance, with lots of singers, or a typical long benefit concert (with countless items, and various different performers) from the nineteenth century?

Another way to limit the scope is to define the key elements of a 'core' record, allowing the input of essential information without cataloguing to the greatest detail. Thus it may not be deemed necessary to index all performers and works, even if this would limit the overall value of the catalogue. The approach taken by cataloguers at the Britten-Pears Library is useful in this respect, since they have identified a body of material for detailed cataloguing (programmes relating directly to performances given by Benjamin Britten and Peter Pears) and treat the remainder at a slightly lower level of disclosure.

Practical considerations

This phase in the project is similar in scope to *Ensemble*, the project to retro-convert catalogue records of printed music, with a view to sharing them via CURL. The model chosen for *Ensemble* involved the collaboration of twelve libraries, with cataloguing taking place in the libraries where collections were held. The use of externally produced electronic records was identified as a way to reduce the in-house cataloguing effort and minimise the need to create records from scratch as much as possible. This distributed model would work in the same way for concert programmes, although very few records may be derived from external databases. The project could start with a small group of representative institutions, such as the British Library, the Bodleian Library and the Royal College of Music. The records created at this initial stage could then be used as the basis for cataloguing other collections in subsequent phases of the project.

Phase 3 of *Ensemble* involved the creation of 72,000 records at an estimated cost of £445,000, of which £360,000 was earmarked for cataloguing and £66,000 was assigned to staffing the project office over a period of two years. The initial phase of the concert programmes project should aim to populate the database with a critical mass of catalogue records, which will involve at least the same overall numbers as *Ensemble*. The project would require large-scale funding over a period of three or more years. The initial focus would necessarily be directed towards cataloguing historical backlogs, but the project definition should also include a realistic appraisal of the cost of an on-going strategy aimed at making the catalogue sustainable in the long-term.

An idea of the scope of such a requirement may be obtained from estimating the number of concerts put on at the South Bank Centre in London every year. The Centre has three performance venues for music: the Royal Festival Hall, the Queen Elizabeth Hall and the Purcell Room. In October 2002, there were a total of 85 musical events at the Centre, of which two were repeated. We can assume that a programme was printed for most, if not all, of these concerts. While this number of concerts is not repeated throughout the year (the summer months of July and August in particular are quiet), it is reasonable to assume that the Centre puts on about eight hundred musical events each year and that a programme is distributed at most of them. Assuming a cataloguing rate of one item per 20 minutes, it would take a full time cataloguer at least seven weeks (at 36 hours per week) to catalogue eight hundred programmes. Other venues that mount professional performances on a regular basis include the Barbican Hall, the Wigmore Hall, St. John's Smith Square, St. Martin-in-the-Fields, the Royal Opera House, and English National Opera. If we add smaller venues, music clubs and societies, and venues in the Greater London area, it may well be that a full-time post is required merely to keep abreast of these programmes and to ensure that a comprehensive collection is maintained, either in one institution or distributed among several partner institutions.

Collection development

A major outcome of the project will make it possible to identify gaps in the programme holdings for concerts and other musical events in UK and Irish libraries generally. The preliminary list of collections given in this report has already thrown up some surprising lacuna, such as the apparent lack of a comprehensive collection of programmes for the Barbican Hall in London. The coverage of many regional venues is also likely to be patchy. Work on the catalogue should go hand-in-hand with developing a cohesive strategy to collect and preserve concert programmes in the UK and Ireland to ensure they are preserved for future generations of researchers. The three main areas to consider are:

A distributed national collection

It may not be practical, or even desirable, to maintain comprehensive collections of programmes at each of the six copyright libraries – indeed, very few programmes are deposited at all of them at present. But it should be possible to co-ordinate collection development policies to make sure that at least one copy is preserved and made available in an appropriate institution. A first step towards achieving this goal is to seek agreement between the copyright libraries to define areas of responsibility.

Legal Deposit

The subject of legal deposit for printed ephemera remains a grey area and very few concert venues currently deposit programmes on a regular basis (the Royal Festival Hall and the Royal Opera House are two exceptions). Formal agreement should be sought with venues, publishers, agents, and ensembles to facilitate the deposit of concert programmes on a regular basis.

Other sources of programmes

There are several other sources of programmes that may be harnessed to improve overall coverage. Music publishers' hire libraries, for example, routinely request copies of concert programmes relating to performances of works in their collections. The Hire Library Committee of the Music

Publishers' Association has indicated an interest to collaborate with the project to ensure the long-term preservation of these programmes. Other agencies that also receive copies of programmes on a regular basis include the Performing Rights Society, *Making Music*, and regional Arts Councils.

8. Summary and Conclusions

Of the five major types of music research materials – manuscripts, printed editions, books on music, music periodicals, and concert programmes – concert programmes represent the last major category of material that has not been subject to any kind of systematic treatment on a national level. They are a valuable resource for music research, teaching and learning. Programmes range in format from loose flyers (printed or manuscript) to bound booklets with analytical notes. They are produced for various types of musical event, including orchestral concerts, opera performances, solo recitals, jazz and pop concerts, musicals, and folk music concerts. Their content offers rich potential for investigation of such diverse topics as performance history, composer and performer biography, the creative process, local history, iconography and institutional history.

Collections of programmes are to be found in a wide variety of library and archival contexts, including public and private archives, local studies libraries, libraries of academic institutions, performance venues, music publishers' archives, and cathedral libraries. In this report, I have identified over one thousand collections of programmes in various institutions in the UK and Ireland, including three hundred collections at the British Library alone. This represents only a small proportion of total resource. The researcher currently has no means of locating collections of programmes other than directing speculative enquiries to likely institutions. The vast majority of collections also remain uncatalogued and remain hidden from the eyes of potential users.

To address this major gap in the coverage of music resources overall, I have recommended a project in two stages. The first objective will be to compile a directory of concert programmes in the UK and Ireland, to be delivered in print and/or electronic format. Building on the work of the *Cecilia* project, the aim of this phase of the project will be to compile a collection level map of concert programmes in different sectors. The successful completion of this phase would facilitate work on the projected Union Catalogue of Concert Programmes, with records at item level. At the same time, steps should be taken to develop a strategy to collect and preserve concert programmes, to address the problem of legal deposit and to outline the framework for distributed national collections of concert programmes in the UK and Ireland.

Appendix 1

Concert Programmes in the UK and Ireland

A preliminary register of collections of programmes by location, giving brief descriptions and relevant contextual information where available.

ABERDEEN

University of Aberdeen

Papers of Bobby Watson, Highland dancer and teacher
Programmes of Highland games, festivals, concerts and other events (1950s-90s).

ALDEBURGH

Britten-Pears Library, Snape

Main collections (mostly filed chronologically): concert and stage performances involving Benjamin Britten and/or Peter Pears (card indexes of Britten's works by work, city, and date); other performances of Britten works, including most first performances (card index by composer and work); programmes in the English Opera Group/English Music Theatre Company archives (1947-81), filed by composer and work; programmes in the Aldeburgh Foundation/Aldeburgh Productions archives, including Aldeburgh Festival and Britten-Pears School events (card index by composer and work, and a less complete card index by artist); programmes in archives of Britten's and Pears's associates, e.g. Joan Cross, Nancy Evans, and Elizabeth Mayer.

BANGOR

University of Wales

Bangor Musical Club (1959-73)

Mary Davies - Welsh Folk Song Society
Letters, articles and a scrapbook. The scrapbook includes press cuttings, articles, and concert programmes (1906-28).

R. D. Griffith Manuscripts
Programmes of oratorio performances conducted by R. D. Griffith at Bethesda and Colwyn Bay (1920-32) and of concerts by the Morfa Rhianedd Orchestra (1940-43).

Rhyd y Meirch Chapel (Cwm Penmachno) Music Festival
Collection includes 7 tickets and 3 programmes (1898-1912).

BEDFORD

Bedford Local Studies Library

Incomplete collection of concert programmes and publicity material relating to the evacuation of the BBC Music Department to Bedford during the Second World War (1941-45). The library also has a small number of documents relating to the Bedford Harmonic Society, including concert programmes, correspondence and corporate/business records (1936-38).

BEDFORDSHIRE

Bedfordshire and Luton Archives and Record Service

BBC Symphony Orchestra
Programmes for concerts given in Bedford during the evacuation of the BBC Music Department to Bedford in World War II. Includes Promenade Concerts and the 'Bedford Farewell Concert'.

Bedford Music Club (1969-84)

Bedford Musical Society (1867-1992)

BIRMINGHAM

Barber Music and Fine Art Library

Barber Institute of Fine Arts concert series (1945-)

Birmingham City Archives

Papers of the Cadbury family of Birmingham
Memorial Hall Temperance Choir (1882)

Birmingham City Museum and Art Gallery

Concert programmes and other musical ephemera relating to Birmingham.

Birmingham Festival Choral Society

Private collection of post-1960 programmes. All items prior to 1960 deposited at Birmingham Central Library, although much archive material was lost in an air raid on Birmingham in 1940. Hand-list detailing programmes, handbills, posters, etc. available.

Birmingham University Information Services, Special Collections Department

Album of Programmes (*ca.*1880-*ca.*1900)
Dramatic and musical entertainments and productions at London theatres and other London venues.

Josef Holbrooke Collection (ca. 1900-1946)
The collection includes various printed items, mainly consisting of concert programmes for performances that Holbrooke was involved in.

Papers of Herman Sutherland Bantock
Concert programmes relating to Herman Bantock (1874-1965), cousin of Sir Granville Bantock. Bantock made his living as a professional violin and viola player, initially in sea-side orchestras such as on Blackpool's North Pier and in the Rimmer String Quartet, and later in the Hallé and Liverpool Philharmonic orchestras.

The Masterman Papers
Scrapbook compiled by Lucy Masterman, mainly during her visit to South Africa, including press cuttings, concert programmes and invitation cards (1902-).

City of Birmingham Symphony Orchestra

The CBSO has an extensive archive of concert programmes and annual prospectuses dating back to its foundation in 1920. The archive holds the vast majority of the Birmingham programmes, but those for 'out-of-town' concerts are thinner on the ground, at least in the early years. Programmes are stored chronologically and are readily accessed in this form, but are not catalogued. The archive also holds a small collection of programmes of non-CBSO concerts. A few of these are from the late nineteenth century, but most date from the 1920s or 1930s and mostly of choral/orchestral concerts promoted by local choral societies, often involving CBSO players.

BOLTON

Bolton Archive and Local Studies Service

Bolton Choral Union (1864-1975, miscellaneous)

Bolton County Borough
Queen's Park concert programmes (1924-25)

Whittle-le-Woods & Clayton-le-Woods
Old Folks' Treat concert programme (13 Nov 1930)

Bolton Central Library

Bolton Amateur Orchestral Society
Bolton Chamber Music Concerts (1930s)
Bolton Chamber Music Society (Drawing Room Concerts, 1895-1913)

Bolton Central Library (cont.)

Bolton Choral Union (programmes and posters: 1895, 1909, 1920, 1929, 1931-55, 1959-60, 1962 and 1975 onwards)
Bolton Festival of Music
Bolton Haydn and Schubert Festival (scrapbook of programmes and newspaper cuttings, 1967)
Bolton Philharmonic Society (1838-44)
Bolton Temperance Progression Society

BOURNEMOUTH

Bournemouth Music Library

Bournemouth Municipal Orchestra, 1895-1934 (nearly complete set).

Bournemouth Reference Library

Grand Theatre (1895, 1904)
New Town Hall (1888-95)
Theatre Royal (1893-1931)
Winter Gardens (1894-1974)

Papers of Sir Dan Godfrey
Scrapbook of press cuttings, programmes and other memorabilia relating to the Bournemouth Municipal Orchestra.

Russell-Cotes Art Gallery and Museum

Archive of the Bournemouth Orchestras consisting of concert programmes, posters, sheet music, photographs and other memorabilia.

BRISTOL

Bristol Record Office

Papers of J.T. Francombe
Concert programmes and orders of service (*ca.*1890-1924)

St. Michael and All Angels Parish, Bedminster
Concert programmes (1963-65)

St. Mary Redcliffe Parish: Papers of Canon E.L.Hertslet
Pamphlets, posters, orders of service, concert programmes, tickets (1928-36).

BRITISH INSTITUTE OF JAZZ STUDIES

Founded in the 1960s, the institute has one of the largest reference collections of jazz literature in the country, including books, magazines, programmes, newspaper cuttings for use by students and researchers.

BROMLEY

Bromley Central Library

Crystal Palace Saturday Concerts, miscellaneous programmes (1884-96)

BUCKINGHAMSHIRE

Buckinghamshire Records and Local Studies Service

Packe of Burnham

Burnham musical society (1923)

BURY

Bury Archive Service

Bury Choral Society

Minute Books, 1953-59, including concert programme (1934)

Stand Lane Independent Church

Annual Concerts (1870-87)

Entertainment and concert programmes (1867-94)

Popular Saturday evening concert programme (1909)

Sunday School Grand Scotch concert programme (1889)

CAMBRIDGE

Cambridge University Library

Walter Bache (1865-88)

Cam Papers

Ephemeral items produced by the University and its societies from their inception to the present. These include leaflets, posters, notices and concert programmes.

Crystal Palace (Oct-Nov 1897)

Royal Promenade Cheltenham Pump & Concert Rooms

Grand vocal and instrumental concerts (1862)

York, Lunatic Asylum

Scrapbook containing newspaper cuttings, concert programmes, trade literature etc., relating mainly to York Lunatic Asylum, Bootham and Barnwood House, Gloucester, collected by Dr F. Needham (*ca.*1860-90).

Cambridge University Library

Department of Manuscripts and University Archives

Cambridge University Musical Club (1889-1990)

Programmes and posters covering concerts given by Cambridge University Musical Club and the Cambridge University Chamber Orchestra. Includes a concert index comprising, for each composer and piece, a note of the date performed.

Cambridge University Rifle Volunteers

Sergeants' Mess minute book (1896-1914), includes smoking concert programmes.

Marten Papers

Printed material, including 2 concert programmes.

Musical Union (London) (1845-67)

Some sets bound as the *Record of the Musical Union.*

Papers and correspondence of Joseph Needham

220th Anniversary of the Academy of Sciences of the USSR, Moscow and Leningrad (15-28 June 1945). Memorabilia, including annotated theatre and concert programmes, etc.

St. John's College

New Musical Society (1880-1975, 11 items)

Records of the Lady Margaret Boat Club

Programmes for smokers and concerts (1825-1958)

Kings College

Kings College Musical Society (1855-2000)

Trinity College

Papers and correspondence of Otto Robert Frisch

Includes loose page of notes on verso of concert programme (1943).

CAVERSHAM

BBC Written Archives Centre

Programmes for concerts given by BBC orchestras and in the BBC Henry Wood Promenade Concerts series.

CHELTENHAM

Cheltenham Art Gallery and Museum

Archive of material relating to Gustav Holst, including a small number of concert programmes and other ephemera.

Cheltenham Arts Festivals

Music Festival programme books with details of concerts, premieres and artists appearing, 1946 onwards.

CHESHIRE

Cheshire and Chester Archives and Local Studies Service

The Cheshire Society in London

Scrapbook (June 1914-March 1926), includes press cuttings, concert programmes and tickets for Society dinners.

Crewe Mechanical Institute

Social club minutes, including various concert programmes (1917-22)

Higher Tranmere, Wesley Chapel

Band of Hope and Temperance Society Minutes

Inserted: lists of members, letters, concert programmes (1896-1938)

Padgate Wesleyan Methodist Chapel

Fisk Jubilee Trio concert programmes (*ca.*1930)

COCKERMOUTH

Cockermouth Harmonic Society

Archive includes about 100 programmes dating from the choir's foundation in 1867 onwards.

GERALD COKE HANDEL COLLECTION

Several hundred programmes of Handel concerts, from the eighteenth century to the present. A large number of programmes for Crystal Palace Handel Festivals and the Halle Handel Festivals. With word-books, playbills, fly-posters, tickets, etc. and a complete set of programmes of the Deal & Walmer Handelian Society, 1946-70.

CORNWALL

Cornwall Record Office

St. Cleer Parish

Church visitors' book (1946-52), originally used as record book for monthly concert programmes (1938-41).

CUMBRIA

Cumbria Record Office and Local Studies Library, Whitehaven

South William Street Church, Workington

Choir report and accounts (1905-06); choir festival poster (1915); concert programme for trust anniversary and harvest festival (1938).

Trinity Methodist Church, Workington

Choir Records (1920-23): attendance register of the Male Voice Choir, with concert programmes.

Workington Methodist Circuit

Chapel Records: Seaton Wesleyan Chapel (1960 and undated)
Sunday School Anniversary concert programmes (MS)

Cumbria Record Office, Carlisle Headquarters

Alston Methodist Church

Concert programme for St. Paul's Methodist Church Alston Young People's Guild (1947)

Carlisle Charlotte Street Congregational Church

Pleasant Sunday Afternoon concert programme on hand-coloured rice paper (1892)

Carlisle Choral Society

Programmes, handbills and correspondence (1885-86, 1897-98, 1927-31)

Carlisle Scouting

Bundle of mementoes of the Scouters' and Guiders' Cruise on S.S. Calgaric (1933), including a concert programme aboard.

Cumberland and Westmorland Association of Tyneside

Bundle containing concert programmes for Carlisle Workshops for the Blind concerts (1936-37), and programme for Eskdale Centre.

Stanwix Choral Society

Miscellaneous papers, including a concert programme autographed by Constance Shacklock (1957).

Cumbria Record Office, Kendal

Kendal Choral Society
Concert programmes and posters (1909-54)

Cumbria Railway Association
Alfred Walker Collection: concert programmes (1845)

DELIUS

Delius Trust

Extensive collection of programmes of concerts and festivals from 1899 onwards containing works by Delius. Programmes are British and foreign and are sorted in chronological order. New items, both new and historical, are added to the collection as they are acquired.

DONCASTER

Doncaster Archives, Doncaster Metropolitan Borough Council

Papers of H.C. Dodds
Mostly records of H. C. Dodds, musician and conductor (born 1903) and his brother, A. B. Dodds (1900-68). Concert programmes (1930s-77).

Doncaster and South Yorkshire Choral Union (1863-81)

DORKING

Leith Hill Music Festival

Private collection. *Ca.*500 programmes for competitions, festival concerts, Children's Days, St. Matthew Passion performances, and special performances (1905-). Hand-list available.

DORSET

Dorset Record Office

Pentridge Church of England Elementary School
Concert programme (1925)

Weymouth Grammar School
Annual concert programmes (1933-35, 1948, 1982)
Summer concert and junior concert programmes (1977-81)

DUBLIN

Christ Church Cathedral, Dublin

Large collections of service sheets which, in recent years, often refer to visiting choirs. Small collection of concert programmes for performances at the Cathedral.

Contemporary Music Centre

Digital collection of programme notes for works by contemporary Irish composers and a collection of original concert programmes.

National Library of Ireland

See Appendix 3.

Trinity College, Dublin

Miscellaneous concert and opera programmes, including Royal Opera House programmes (1979-).

Trinity College Singers, Dublin

Concert programmes (1949-, lacking 1953-61 and 1969-74).

DUNDEE

Central Library, Local Studies Department

Several thousand concert programmes dating from 1860 to the 1940s. Sorted into year order and, where applicable, into concert series sequence. Programmes for concerts, *conversaziones* and other miscellaneous musical events spread throughout the collection of general Victoriana, because they were hosted by a particular local club or were part of week-long fund-raising festivals or bazaars for volunteer companies or churches. A few programmes have been selected for digitisation as part of a wider programme (including programmes of Dundee recitals given by Sarasate, Bottesini, Joachim and Ysaÿe).

DURHAM

Durham University Library

Else Headlam-Morley Collection (ca.1880-1950)

Manuscript and printed scores of Lady Headlam-Morley's compositions, correspondence, concert programmes, posters and press cuttings, and other papers and photographs.

EDINBURGH

National Library of Scotland

See Appendix 3.

Edinburgh Central Library

Patterson's Concerts (*ca.*1890-1900)

Usher Hall: miscellaneous concert programmes, including concerts given by the Scottish Orchestra (1938-40)

Edinburgh City Libraries: Music Library

Edinburgh International Festival: late nineteenth century to date, with composer/title index to 1980s.

Musical Union (London), 1847-69.

Edinburgh University Library

Edinburgh International Club
Includes a file containing historical information about the Club, cuttings, membership cards, and programmes of events.

Edinburgh Royal Choral Union (1940s-)

Reid Orchestral Concerts (1915-)
With programme notes by Sir Donald Tovey.

Tovey Collection
Material relating to the life and work, musical writings and compositions of Sir Donald Tovey, including miscellaneous concert programmes.

ELGAR

Elgar Birthplace Museum

Collection of concert programmes and press cuttings

Elgar Society

Collection of concert programmes.

EXETER

Devon Record Office

Newport Parish
Church concert programme in aid of building the fund (3 Feb 1965).

Saint Luke's College
Bundle of theatre and concert programmes (*ca.*1960-70).

Uffculme Parish
Scrapbook containing newspaper cuttings, concert programmes, verses, etc., compiled by Alice Marker (1866-86).

GLASGOW

Glasgow University Library Music Collection

Programmes relating mainly to Scottish institutions, dating from *ca.*1870 to the present. Societies represented include the Clydebank Choral Union Glasgow Cathedral Choral Society, Glasgow Chamber Music Society, Glasgow Choral Union, Glasgow University Orchestral Society, Greenock Orchestral Society, Stirling Amateur Orchestral Society and the Strolling Players Amateur Orchestral Society. Also holds a collection of programmes for the Concerts of Ancient Music (1779-1845).

Glasgow University Library, Special Collections Department

Papers and compositions of William Beatton Moonie (1910-1961)

Concert programmes including works by William Moonie 1913-45

Records of Scottish Ballet (1957-99)

Programmes, photographs, leaflets, periodicals, press cuttings, posters and other papers relating to the Scottish Ballet and Western Ballet Theatre.

Glasgow University Archive

Royal Scottish Academy of Music & Drama and predecessor institutions

Programme and press cutting volumes (1886-1955)

Concert and performance programmes (1931-84)

Royal Scottish Academy of Music and Drama

Some uncatalogued programmes of operas from Glasgow and London, plus a few turn-of-the-century programmes from a Glasgow series (also uncatalogued).

GLOUCESTER

Gloucestershire Record Office

R. A. J. (Jack) Bell of Lydney

Records collected and compiled by Jack Bell relating to aspects of local history, including programmes, notices and press cuttings of various sporting, cultural and other events in Lydney (1947-85). Includes Lydney Congregational Choral Society's concert programmes (1947-49), and a celebration of Herbert Howells's 90th birthday (1982).

Gloucester Methodist Circuit

Chapel Records, Tibberton: concert programmes (1965-68)

Gloucestershire Record Office (cont.)

Gloucestershire Quarter Sessions
Gloucestershire Police Records: Haw bridge murder enquiry (1938)
Items taken from Tower Lodge, Leckhampton and 248 Old Bath Road, Cheltenham, including hand-printed concert programme 'The Wright Party'.

Hillview County Primary School, Hucclecote
Various school play and concert programmes, 1963-84.

Kathleen Norman collection
Handbook and concert programmes for Gloucester City Education Week (1933).

Old Chapel Congregational Church, Stroud
Miscellaneous bazaar and concert programmes (1884-97)

Rodborough Tabernacle
Miscellaneous papers (1908-86), including orders of service, concert programmes and handbills.

Tewkesbury High School for Girls
Play and concert programmes (1953-70)

GLYNDEBOURNE

Glyndebourne Festival Opera Archive
Glyndebourne Festival Opera (1934-)
Glyndebourne Touring Opera (1968-)

HAMPSHIRE

Hampshire Record Office

Austen-Leigh Family
Items found inside the Diaries of Emma Austen-Leigh (1801-76): programme for 'Mrs Dixon's concert', 1820; concert programme possibly in the hand of Augusta Smith, n.d.; concert programme for Winterbourn School including a reading by Arthur Austen-Leigh (1876).

Bonham Carter Family
Gerard Bonham Carter: miscellaneous letters and papers (1897-1910), including concert programmes at Hatfield Heath (1897).

Joanna Francis Bonham Carter: miscellaneous letters found loose with Joan Bonham Carter's letters to her brother Gerard, with 5 concert programmes (1863-1940).

Hampshire Record Office (cont.)

Theatrical Collection

Barton Peveril College, Eastleigh (1952-92.)

Basingstoke Concert Club (1975-99)

Blanche Wills Chandler Papers (programmes and playbills for performances in Hampshire and London, 1867-1908)

Hampshire Rural Music School (1934-75)

King Alfred's College, Winchester (1932-80s)

Queenswood College Mutual Improvement Society (1852-92, scrapbook)

Winchester Amateur Operatic Society (1912-90s)

Winchester City Festival Choir (1923-93)

HEREFORD

Herefordshire Record Office

Hampton Court Estate

Chamber concert programmes (1866, 1869, 1872, 1874-77, 1879-80, 1882-83, 1885-87, 1889-90, 1892-94)

Charity concert programmes (1882-98)

Concert programmes (1863-78)

Evening concert programme at Oswestry (1873)

Hand written concert programmes for Shobdon Rectory Schoolroom (1863-78)

Morning concert programmes (1864-91, 1892 (April only), 1893-98)

HERTFORD

Hertfordshire Archives and Local Studies

Hatfield and Welwyn Garden City Development Corporation

Welwyn Garden City Music Society concert programme (Dec 1925)

HUDDERSFIELD

Huddersfield Public Library, Local Studies Library

Extensive collection of concert ephemera.

Tolston Memorial Museum

Concert programmes, music and other printed ephemera.

HULL

Hull City Archives

The Hull Daily Mail Collection

Hull Choral Union (1934-39)

Hull Philharmonic Orchestra (1934-39)

KEELE

University of Keele, Music Department Library

Collection of archival material pertaining to the life of the composer Havergal Brian, including concert programmes.

KENDAL

Cumbria Record Office, Kendal

Cumbria Railway Association
Third Annual Smoking Concert programme (3 Dec 1921)

Stricklandgate Methodist Church
Grand concert programme (26 Feb 1949)

KENT

Bexley Local Studies and Archive Centre

Records of Chislehurst and Sidcup Grammar School
Concert programmes, correspondence, etc. (1955-66)
Scrapbook (1979-80) includes concert programmes

LANCASHIRE

Lancashire Record Office

Blackpool Glee and Madrigal Society
Programme for a concert at the Hotel Metropole (3 May 1923)
Souvenir silk programme, Blackpool Winter Gardens (18 June 1880)

Blackpool Musical Festival (1884-1948)

Burnley Baptist Churches' Records
Angle Street Baptist Church, Golden Jubilee: tea, pageant and concert programme (2 June 1928).

Lancaster Orchestral Society (n.d., 1955, 1957)

Walton United Reformed Church, Liverpool (concert programme, 1972)

LEEDS

Leeds University Library

J. H. Birkinshaw papers
7 concert and theatre programmes in English, French and Russian (1917).

Ernest Bradbury
Music critic for the *Yorkshire Post*, collection of programmes (1940s-80s)

Mark Lavery collection
Leningrad, Moscow, and Riga concert programmes (1961-78)

Oliver Locker-Lampson papers
British Armoured Cars concert programme (20 May 1916).

Henry Pattman papers
Held as a POW at Limburg: concert programmes (10-12 Sept 1917)

Bernard Percival papers
Held as a POW at Pforzheim from April 1918: concert programme (8 Oct 1918)

Ruhleben POWs: Papers of British soldiers interned at Ruhleben Concentration Camp during the First World War

H. Richard Lorenz
Chamber concert programme (23 Oct 1917)
Tercentenary Shakespeare Festival programme (23-25 April 1916)

Harold Redmayne
17 Ruhleben theatre and concert programmes (1915-18)

Alfred Salomon
Extensive collection of printed theatre and concert programmes, revue extracts, poems and song-sheets (1914-18).

William Swale
Printed theatre and concert programmes, revue extracts, poems and song-sheets (1915-17); Tercentenary Shakespeare Festival song-sheet (23-30 April 1916); manuscript verses of the Ruhleben song and 5 other songs (n.d.).

E. R. Vincent
3 concert programmes (8 Jan 1916, n.d.)

Leeds University Library (cont.)

Evgenii Sablin papers (1875-1949)
Concert and exhibition programmes concerning Russian welfare and religious institutions in London.

Herbert Thompson Collection
A collection of 262 opera, concert and other music programmes assembled by Herbert Thompson, some annotated by him, 1876-1936. Thompson was music and art critic for the *Yorkshire Post* (from 1886) and Yorkshire correspondent of the *Musical Times*. He retired from the *Yorkshire Post* in 1936.

Leeds College of Music
Small specialist jazz collection, including programmes of Duke Ellington concerts at Leeds. College archival programmes dating from the 1960s.

LIVERPOOL

University of Liverpool

Memorabilia of voyage on the Royal George
Programme of concert held on board (27 Sept 1919).

Memorabilia from voyages on board Etruria
Programmes of evening concerts held on board the Etruria (19 March 1892 and 27 April 1892).

Royal Liverpool Philharmonic Orchestra (Boardroom)
Programmes (*ca.*1860 to date)

Dorothy Stephenson, student papers (1907-35)
Miscellaneous concert programmes

Dora Yates Collection
Printed programmes, etc., including programme of Liverpool Teachers' Guild concert (12 Jan 1889).

LONDON

BBC Music Library

Constant Lambert Collection

Includes programmes of performances of William Walton's Façade (1920-29).

Libretti Collection

The collection largely consists of nineteenth and twentieth century published libretti. Many relate to specific performances, including those given at The Royal Opera House, Covent Garden, the Theatre Royal, Drury Lane, and The Kings Theatre, Haymarket. These were originally performed by a variety of companies, including the Royal Italian Opera Company and the Carl Rosa Opera Company. Concert programmes, many relate to specific performances, listing performers and performance details.

Boosey & Hawkes Music Publishers Ltd

Boosey & Hawkes Ballad Concerts (1864-1939)

The British Library

See Appendix 2.

Conway Hall, Red Lion Square

South Place Concerts (established 1887)

Imperial War Museum Department of Documents

Lieutenant Colonel A W Shirley TD

Scrapbook (in 4 tan rexin bound volumes)

Invitations, menus, greeting cards and concert programmes, hand drawn/printed by prisoners in the camps or fellow officers etc.

Dr G H Bickmore

Photocopy of his memoir covering his service as a junior paymaster officer in HMS Warspite. Three original ship's concert programmes from 1916 to 1918 are preserved with the memoir.

Flying Officer R J Fayers

Miscellaneous POW papers, including concert programmes (1943-45).

Jewish Music Institute Library

The JMI Library holds programmes of JMI performances of music of Jewish interest and significance. These include programmes of the biennial Jewish Music Festivals 1984-2000. Each festival includes 20-50 concerts, recitals, illustrated lectures and seminars at various London venues and some provincial cities, including the Barbican, South Bank, St. John's Smith Square, York Minster, Canterbury Cathedral and St. Paul's Cathedral as well as synagogues, universities and churches. The music includes sacred, ethnic, folk and art music from the different communities where Jews have settled across the globe over the last 3,000 years. Ongoing programmes include themed days of Jewish music at the South Bank with 6 events in the Purcell Room and Queen Elizabeth Hall each November. JMI concert programmes also include music by composers banned, exiled and killed by the Nazi Regime, such as *Thwarted Voices: Music Suppressed by the Third Reich*, 6 concerts on the South bank November 2001 and *Continental Britons – the Émigré Composers* two concerts at the Wigmore Hall in June 2002'. JMI also holds programmes of Jewish music presented by other organisations.

King's College London Archives Services

King's College London Department of Music Records
Concert programmes and departmental prospectuses (1966-85).

The London Library

A small number of concert programmes relating to several national events, including Coronations and the Festival of Britain.

London Metropolitan Archives

Cook Collection of 19th century theatrical papers (1855-68)
Programmes, advertisements, playbills, libretti, guides and catalogues to theatrical and musical performances in London establishments, including Royal English Opera House, Covent Garden; Royal Italian Opera House, Covent Garden; Royal Academy of Music; Weston's Grand Music Hall; Crystal Palace.

City of London Maternity Hospital
Concert programme and playbill for performances held in aid of the hospital.

Codd family (1824-1901)
Folder of miscellaneous papers, including concert programmes.

Holy Trinity Church, Haverstock Hill: Clarence Way, Camden
Parish magazines (concert programmes and tickets pasted in at rear), 1892.

London Metropolitan Archives (cont.)

Royal Choral Society Archive
Near-complete run of concert programmes.

St. Alban The Martyr, Holborn: Brook Street, Camden
Concert programme in aid of St. Martin's League, embodying report for 1890 (31 Jan 1892).

Uxbridge Choral Society Archive
Concert programmes and posters (1925-92)

Wolley Family
Concert programme at Ilchester (1884)

London Symphony Orchestra Archive
Complete set of programmes of LSO concerts.

Serge Prokofiev Archive (Goldsmiths College, London)
Programmes of Prokofiev's performances in London dating from the late 1920s, plus his appearances in the US, France and Russia. The archive also collects programmes relating to premiere performances.

Richmond Concert Society
Complete private collection of society programmes (1962-). Also holds a selection of Crystal Palace concert programmes from the 1880s, including 'a concert attended by Liszt and a Memorial Concert to Liszt'.

Royal Academy of Music
Birmingham Musical Festival (1900, 1903, 1906, 1912)
Cambridge, New Theatre (14-18 Feb 1928; 14-18 Feb 1931)
Cardiff, Second Cardiff Triennial Musical Festival (1895)
Dundee, Kinnaird Hall (6 Feb 1885)
Elgar Festival (12 June 1949)
Glasgow, The Choral and Orchestral Union of Glasgow, various programmes (1923-29)
Glyndebourne Festival Opera (1952-96)
Guildford, Western Hall (26 May 1887)
Leeds Saturday Orchestral Concerts, miscellaneous (1923-32)
London
Brixton Hall, Alice Aloof's Subscription concerts (25 November 1884)
Buckingham Palace: 30 miscellaneous royal programmes (1843-1900)

Royal Academy of Music (cont.)

London (cont.)

Coliseum: English National Opera (1969-90, incomplete collection)

Concerts of Ancient Music (1786, 1821-1824, 1825, 1826-1830, 1831, 1832-1837, 1838, 1839-1840, 1842-46)

Covent Garden, Royal Italian Opera (2 July 1889)

London Musical Festival (1899-1902, 1911)

Mansion House, London Sunday School Choir (12 May 1893)

Philharmonic Society concerts (1871, 24 Feb 1881–22 June 1889)

Purcell Operatic Society (May 1900, March 1901)

Queen's Hall

Guildhall School of Music Orchestral Concert (22 May 1930)

London Symphony Orchestra, 29th series (1920-1934/35, incomplete)

Symphony Concerts (1897-1927, and miscellaneous loose copies 1903-7, 1930-35)

Symphony Concerts Ysaÿe & Busoni (1900-01)

Symphony Concerts Wagner & Ysaÿe (1898-1900)

Sunday Afternoon Concerts (1897-1905)

Sunday Afternoon Orchestral Concerts (1896-97)

Sunday Chamber Concerts (1896-97)

Sunday Concerts (1905-24)

Sunday Evening Concerts (1898-99)

Royal Academy of Music concerts (1825-, incomplete)

Royal Albert Hall: miscellaneous programmes

Henry Wood Promenade Concerts (1895-1927)

Manchester

Brand Lane Festival Concerts (1919-23, miscellaneous)

Brand Lane Orchestral and Celebrity Concerts (1925-26, miscellaneous)

Brand Lane Orchestral Concerts (1913-23 miscellaneous)

Brand Lane Subscription Concerts (1916-17)

Sir Charles Hallé's concerts in Manchester (30 Jan 1858–7 March 1895)

Meiningen Orchestra concert programmes, St. James's Hall (1902)

Newman's Concert Programmes (1901-02)

Norfolk & Norwich Musical Festival (1830)

Norfolk & Norwich Centenary Triennial Musical Festival (1905, 1908, 1911, 1924, 1927, 1930)

Osborne: 2 royal programmes (1854, 1856)

Richter Concerts (29 June 1891)

Windsor, St. George's Hall: 7 miscellaneous royal programmes (1844-66)

Royal Academy of Music (cont.)

Henry Wood's collections of 'Miscellaneous concert programmes':

London (1901-12)
Provincial (1904-12)
London & Provincial (1934-37)
Henry Wood Promenade Concerts (various)

Extensive collection of eighteenth and nineteenth century programmes in archive of the music agent Norman McCann, acquired in 1999.

Royal Albert Hall

Archive of programmes associated with the Hall.

Royal College of Music
Department of Portraits and Performance History

The programmes collection currently amounts to some 600,000 items ranging from 1780 to the present day; although international in scope its bias is inevitably towards the UK and especially London. Storage is normally by venue—the hand-list lists 1064 locations for London alone—but numerous special collections, such as those of Arthur Jacobs, Léon Goossens, Ivor Newton and André Mangeot, maintain their own integrity. The Ibbs and Tillett archive embraces ledgers, correspondence and an important sequence of London recital programmes from 1923 to 1945. Long runs include:

Monday and Saturday Popular Concerts
BBC Symphony Concerts
Boston Symphony Orchestra
Concerts of Ancient Music
Courtauld-Sargent Concerts
Crystal Palace Saturday Concerts
Glasgow Choral Union
Hallé Orchestra
Musical Union
Philharmonic Society
Queen's Hall Symphony and Sunday Concerts
RCM concerts
Richter Concerts
Sacred Harmonic Society

Card indices of artists, first performances, orchestra lists, subscriber lists and iconographical content cover most of the collection up to 1960 and additional

Royal College of Music (cont.)

fields in the new online catalogue include venue, concert type, instrument, choir lists, agents, programme note writers, and presence of reviews, annotations or tickets.

The departmental reference library has a substantial performance history section with histories of halls, theatres and societies; approximately 500 images of halls and opera houses figure in the print and photograph collection. An index of obituaries in music periodicals provides a quick route to information on many obscure performers.

Royal College of Music Library

Crystal Palace Saturday Concerts
Miscellaneous programmes, with Sir George Grove's annotations

Special collections that include programmes:
Stanley Bate (*ca.*1948-58)
Graham Carritt (1934-37)
Dolmetsch Family (1929-80)
Thomas Frederick Dunhill (mainly 1931-40)
Katharine Goodson (1911-20)
Herbert Howells: concert programmes with notes by Howells.
Basil Lam: Promenade Concerts series programme notes (1962-81); programmes for concerts by the Basil Lam Sonata Ensemble (1946-54).
Charles Thornton Lofthouse (1950s-70s)
Society of Women Musicians (1911-72)

Royal College of Organists Library

Musical Union (London) (1854-81)

Royal Festival Hall Archive

Concert programmes (May 1951-, incomplete)
Monthly diaries (May 1951-)
Card index of works and artists (1951-84)
Computer listing of works and artists (Sept 1993-; no public access)
Posters (mainly from 1986)
Leaflets/handbills (1986-)

Royal Opera House Archive

Programmes, press cuttings, etc.

Royal Philharmonic Society Archive

Concert programmes (1813-)

Trinity College of Music

Programmes of College performances and some major collections of concert programmes, acquired largely by donation. College also houses the Mander and Mitchenson Theatre Collection, which includes concert and operatic ephemera.

University College London
School of Slavonic and East European Studies (SSEES) Library

Glenny Collection

Theatre and concert programmes from Moscow and Leningrad (1961-76) and for British performances of plays, ballets or music by Russian writers (1972-88).

Westminster Abbey

Programmes for concerts held at the Abbey and at St. Margaret's Church, Westminster. The programmes are bound up in volumes with service sheets, many of which also have a high musical content (1847 onwards, complete from 1901).

Wigmore Hall Archive

Concert programmes of Bechstein Hall and the Wigmore Hall.

LOUGHTON
The National Jazz Foundation Archive

The Archive is a unique national research and information centre available to jazz enthusiasts, historians, journalists and the general public. Based at Loughton Library in Essex, the Archive houses a valuable collection of rare books, periodicals, photographs and jazz memorabilia. The emphasis is on British materials, but there are also foreign works, particularly American.

LUTON
Luton Central Library

Luton Girls Choir Archive.

MANCHESTER

Hallé Concerts Society Archive

Concert programmes (1858-).

Manchester University

Labour History Archives and Study Centre

Archives of the Communist Party of Great Britain (CPGB)

Russian concert programme, with press cuttings in Russian and English (1959).

Royal Northern College of Music

The Adolph Brodsky Collection

The Russian violinist Adolph Brodsky (1851-1929) was Principal of the Royal Manchester College of Music from 1895 until his death. Concert programmes and press cuttings relating to performances by Brodsky and the Brodsky Quartet.

Papers of Philip Newman, violinist (1917-90)

Letters, photographs, press cuttings, invitations, programmes and artefacts of the violinist Philip Newman. The papers cover his whole career as a concert soloist and teacher, which was forged largely overseas – notably in Belgium and Portugal.

Royal Manchester College of Music Archives (*1893-1973*)

Records include programmes of concerts given by students.

Henry Watson Music Library

Classical Chamber Music Society (1852-58)

Concerts of Ancient Music (1783-1845)

Crystal Palace Saturday Concerts (1867-94)

Hallé Orchestra

(Royal) Liverpool Philharmonic Orchestra (1875-91)

Liverpool Hall Subscription Concerts (1868-93)

Liverpool Musical Festival (1794, 1827, 1830, 1833, 1836)

Monday Popular Concerts (St. James's Hall) (1859-75)

Musical Union (London) (1845-60)

MIDDLESBROUGH

Middlesbrough Central Library Theatrical Collection

Feli Corbett's Subscription Series (1909-33)

Grand Theatre and Opera House programmes (nineteeth century)

Middlesbrough Musical Union (1882-*ca.*1920)

Middlesbrough Operatic Society (1948-76)

NELSON

Nelson and District Choral Society

Concert programmes and annual reports (1908-61)
Programmes from 1961-62 onwards are scattered among society members.

NEWCASTLE

Newcastle City Library

Alderson and Brentnall Concert Programmes (1876-93)
Alderson's Choir (1879-89)
Band Concerts in Newcastle-upon-Tyne (1900-22)
Barras Bridge Assembly Rooms (1889-1912)
Broken Doll: Events (1991-)
Celebrity Concerts in Newcastle-upon-Tyne (1860-1923)
Chamber Music Society, Newcastle-upon-Tyne (1883-1934, 1946-)
City Hall, Newcastle: posters, excluding Northern Sinfonia Concerts (1967-)
City Hall, Newcastle (1929-, incomplete)
Classical Concert Society, Newcastle-upon-Tyne (1907-14)
Conservatoire of Music, Newcastle-upon-Tyne (1898-1929)
Durham University, King's College, Newcastle-upon-Tyne, Choral Society (1908-30, incomplete)
Durham, Northumberland & Newcastle Botanical and Horticultural Society Shows: Music programmes (1878-94)
Fenham and District Amateur Operatic Society (1961-65)
Forest Hill and District Amateur Operatic Society (1938-39, 2 programmes)
Gosforth United Reformed Church, Musical Society (1965-69, 1971-)
Harrison, Percy: Harrison concerts (1897-1916)
Heaton Grammar School, Musical and Dramatic Society (1951, 1953, 1954, 1958)
Laing Art Gallery, Newcastle-upon-Tyne: Lunch Hour Concerts (1941-47)
Music at the People's: programmes and leaflets (1972-)
Musical Events in Newcastle: posters (excluding City Hall events) (1975-)
Musicians' Union Benevolent Fund Concerts (1900-18, incomplete)
Musicon: Durham University Concert Series (1993-)
Newcastle Amateur Vocal Society (1875-1905)
Newcastle and Gateshead Choral Union: programmes and prospectuses (1896-1982, incomplete; between 1889-96 called Gateshead Choral Society)
Newcastle Bach Choir (1916-)
Newcastle Corporation City Hall, vol.1a (1955-67)
Newcastle Corporation, Concerts in the Parks (1962-78, incomplete)
Newcastle Glee and Madrigal Society (1908-36, incomplete)
Newcastle Harmonic Society (1892-1912)
Newcastle Philharmonic Orchestra (1910-34)

SOUTHAMPTON

University of Southampton Libraries Special Collections

Papers of the Gordon family
Including concert programmes and other memorabilia collected by Mildred Katherine Leith, late nineteenth and early twentieth century.

Papers of M.J.Landa relating to the 'Jewish regiment'
The collection includes programmes for performances by supporters of the regiment in aid of the 'comforts fund' and in aid of the Distressed Polish Jews Fund (1915-18), and balance sheet for concerts at the Hackney Empire (1918).

Waley family papers
Twentieth century papers include concert programmes and table plan of the dinner of the Worshipful Company of Musicians (1936).

STALYBRIDGE

Tameside Archive Service

Ashton-under-Lyne Philharmonic Society (1890)
Denton Brass Band (1974-80)
Godley Operatic Society (1926-30)
Pelican Stage Society of Hyde and Gee Cross Wesleyan Church (1927-55)

SUFFOLK

Suffolk Record Office, Bury St. Edmunds Branch

Nayland Choral Society Concert programmes (1911)

Suffolk Record Office, Ipswich Branch

The East Anglian Magazine Photographic Archive
Concert programme (n.d.)

Rowley of Tendring Hall
Colchester Conservative Association concert programmes (1883)

SURREY

Surrey History Centre

Lucy Broadwood Papers
Leith Hill Music Festival: schedules and programmes (1924, 1928-29)

Sir Gervas Powell Glyn, 6th Baronet of Ewell
Album including programmes for music evenings at Rectory House, Ewell (1863-1921).

Leith Hill Music Festival (miscellaneous)
Long Grove Hospital, Epsom (1907-57; 12 programmes)

NORTHUMBERLAND

Northumberland County Record Office

Organ Records

Documents relating to organs in churches and other venues, including letters, papers, patents, photographs, posters, and concert and recital programmes.

NORWICH

Norwich Cathedral, Dean and Chapter Library

Programmes of concerts given at Norwich Cathedral and elsewhere by the Norwich Cathedral Choir and visiting choirs. Also programmes of organ recitals, visiting ensembles and of concerts in the Norfolk and Norwich Triennial Musical Festival.

OLDHAM

Oldham Local Studies and Archives

Oldham Lyceum, School of Music

OXFORD

Bodleian Library, Oxford

Special Collections and Western Manuscripts

Concerts of Ancient Music (1785, 1787-98, 1801-04, 1806, 1813-14, 1816-18, 1821-26, 1828, 1846, 1848)

Papers of Sir John Cowdery Kendrew, molecular biologist
Section R, biographical folders: concert programmes (1944-45)

Records of Various Oxford Music Organisations (1918-76)
Oxford Orchestral Society; Oxford Subscription Concerts; Oxford Chamber Orchestra; Oxford Ladies Musical Society; Oxford Festival of Music.

Records of the Oxfordshire Music Festival
Festival programmes (1945-59)

Oxford Ladies Musical Society
Programmes (1898-1954)

John Johnson Collection of printed ephemera

Collection assembled by John de Monins Johnson between *ca.*1923 and 1956 and was housed at the Oxford University Press until its transfer to the Bodleian Library in 1968. The collection includes 15 boxes of concert programmes for London,

Bodleian Library (cont.)

provincial and foreign venues dating from the eighteenth century to the 1950s. A collection description is available at http://www.bodley.ox.ac.uk/johnson/. Principal London venues include:

Æolian Hall, Bond Street (1902-23)
BBC Henry Wood Promenade Concerts (1929-58)
BBC Symphony Orchestra (1930-44)
Bechstein Hall, later Wigmore Hall (1904-14; 1917-57)
Central Hall, Westminster (1920-49)
Covent Garden (1882-1947)
Crystal Palace (1868-93)
Exeter Hall (1836-69)
Goldsmiths Hall (1925)
Grocers Hall (1921-28)
Hanover Square Rooms
(*later*) Kings Concert Rooms
(*later*) Queens Concert Room (1776-1874)
Mansion House (1871-1910)
Merchant Taylors Hall (1871-1912)
Queen's Hall (1894-?)
Royal Albert Hall (1876-1951)
Royal Festival Hall (1951-60)
St. James's Hall (1858-1904)
St. Saviour's Mission Hall (1887-89)
Steinway Hall, Wigmore Street (1890-1908), became Grotrian Hall (1932)
Victoria and Albert Museum (1951-58)

Principal Oxford venues and societies:

Assembly Rooms (1899-1930)
Corn Exchange (1896-1901)
Exeter College
Holywell Music Room (1792-1953)
Magdalen College
Merton College
New College
Oxford University Musical Club
Sheldonian Theatre (1818-1965)
St. John's College
Town Hall (1828-1933)
Worcester College

Oxford University Music Faculty Library

Beethoven Quartett Society (London) (1845)
Concerts of Ancient Music (1783-1848)

PETERSFIELD

Petersfield Orchestra

Private collection of programmes from 1979 (3 per year). Programme details (from 1972) held in an Access database.

PLYMOUTH

Plymouth and West Devon Record Office

Devonport High School for Boys
Includes: memorial concert programme (1974-75)

Plymouth Corporation: papers of Alderman H G Mason
Novorossisk USSR: City Council Delegation (1956)
Miscellaneous concert programmes, airline ticket and map of Russia.

READING

University of Reading

Centre for Ephemera Studies

Programmes, bills, posters, music covers and trade literature.

Main Library, Whiteknights

Archives
Concert programmes of the Department of Music.

John Lewis Collection
*Ca.*450 examples of music ephemera (1750-), including material relating to the Aldeburgh Festival.

Elspeth Evans Collection
London concert ephemera, including programmes (1970-90)

Finzi Book Room
Programmes of events held in the room.

Music Library

The Finzi Collection: programmes collected by Gerald Finzi.

RHYL

Rhyl Music Club

Archive of *ca.* 700 programmes, including:
Opera for All, miscellaneous
Rhyl Music Club (1947-, some individual programmes missing)
Rhyl Pavilion (1950s and 1960s)
Rhyl Town Hall (1980s and 1990s)
Welsh National Opera, touring programmes

Royal Tunbridge Wells Symphony Orchestra

Orchestra founded in 1922; near-complete collection of programmes from 1929 onwards. There are usually 6 concerts per season, which have taken place since 1936 in the Assembly Hall, Royal Tunbridge Wells.

SEATON

Seaton & District Music Club, Devon

Concert programmes (1952-)

SHEFFIELD

Sheffield Archives

Lyceum theatre (programmes of concerts by the London Philharmonic Orchestra, 1942)
Sheffield Philharmonic Society (concert programmes and press cuttings, 1948-51)
Sheffield University (concert programmes, 1950-56)

SHROPSHIRE

Shropshire Records and Research Centre

The More Collection
Concert programmes and church restoration papers (mainly nineteenth century).

SOMERSET

Bath and North East Somerset Record Office

Diaries and programmes of events in Bath (1870-1936)
Including concert programmes for 1907 and 1912.

Somerset Archive and Record Service

Bridgwater Methodist Circuit records
Concert programme n.d. (probably *ca.*1914-18)

Chard Congregational Church records
Nonconformist United Schools Centenary Concert Programme (1880)

Somerset Archive and Record Service (cont.)

Crewkerne Grammar School records
Play and concert programmes (1927-52)

Diocese of Bath and Wells
Minutes of the Wells Branch of the Church of England Temperance Society, (1885-1911). With press cuttings, concert programmes, etc., inserted.

Edward Jeboult of Taunton
Photocopies (taken at Somerset Record Office) and photographs from MS family history and scrapbook (1890), including John Comer's Subscription Concert Programme (Taunton, 1846).

Somerset Archaeological and Natural History Society Collection
Papers from the collection of Charles Tite
Service programme for the opening of a new church organ in South Petherton (1834); concert programmes: Haselbury Plucknett (1891, 1893); Hambridge (1892); Crewkerne (1891); Rimpton (1893); Princes' Hall (1889, place not stated).

Somerset County Council records
Miscellaneous papers including speech day programmes and headmistress' reports, concert programmes, photographs (1910-72).

Sidcot School records
School Centenary sports, school camps and concert programmes (1908-41).

Taunton
Miscellaneous concert programmes from Taunton, and memorabilia related to the Minehead area (1890-1928).

Thornfalcon Parish
Concert programme, and notice, in aid of school funds (1890).

SORABJI

The Sorabji Archive
Programmes of concerts of Sorabji's music.

SOUTHAMPTON

University of Southampton Libraries Special Collections

Papers of the Gordon family
Including concert programmes and other memorabilia collected by Mildred Katherine Leith, late nineteenth and early twentieth century.

Papers of M.J.Landa relating to the 'Jewish regiment'
The collection includes programmes for performances by supporters of the regiment in aid of the 'comforts fund' and in aid of the Distressed Polish Jews Fund (1915-18), and balance sheet for concerts at the Hackney Empire (1918).

Waley family papers
Twentieth century papers include concert programmes and table plan of the dinner of the Worshipful Company of Musicians (1936).

STALYBRIDGE

Tameside Archive Service

Ashton-under-Lyne Philharmonic Society (1890)
Denton Brass Band (1974-80)
Godley Operatic Society (1926-30)
Pelican Stage Society of Hyde and Gee Cross Wesleyan Church (1927-55)

SUFFOLK

Suffolk Record Office, Bury St. Edmunds Branch

Nayland Choral Society Concert programmes (1911)

Suffolk Record Office, Ipswich Branch

The East Anglian Magazine Photographic Archive
Concert programme (n.d.)

Rowley of Tendring Hall
Colchester Conservative Association concert programmes (1883)

SURREY

Surrey History Centre

Lucy Broadwood Papers
Leith Hill Music Festival: schedules and programmes (1924, 1928-29)

Sir Gervas Powell Glyn, 6th Baronet of Ewell
Album including programmes for music evenings at Rectory House, Ewell (1863-1921).

Leith Hill Music Festival (miscellaneous)
Long Grove Hospital, Epsom (1907-57; 12 programmes)

SUSSEX

East Sussex County Record Office

Lewes Town Band (1914-50)

West Sussex County Record Office

The Goodwood Estate Archives

Charlotte (Gordon), Duchess of Richmond

Guest lists and MS concert programmes (1837, n.d.)

SWANSEA

University of Wales Swansea LIS Archives

Henry Leyshon Collection

Collection includes: order of service for a memorial service for Queen Victoria at the Albert Hall, Swansea (1901); programme of memorial concert for Queen Victoria held at Swansea market (1901).

TEESSIDE

Teesside Archives

Pennyman Family of Ormesby Hall

Miscellaneous family poems, sermons, lecture notes, concert programmes, dance cards (1880-1930). Concert programmes for *Pimpinone*, *Il Ballo Delle Ingrate*, and *The Music Party* (1955).

WARRINGTON

Warrington Reference Library

Warrington Male Voice Choir: concert programmes (1924-96); details of artists and concerts (1973-74).

WARWICKSHIRE

Modern Records Centre, University of Warwick

Vellum Binders' Trade Society (1894)

Warwickshire County Record Office

Papers of Hubert Gerald Holbeche

Bundle of papers containing photographs, concert programmes, press cuttings, etc. (*ca.*1904-35).

WEST BROMWICH

Sandwell Community History and Archives Service

C. J. B. Powell, Smethwick

Press cuttings, correspondence, concert programmes (for Smethwick Choral Society and Orchestra, and the Smethwick Symphony Orchestra) and other ephemera (1888-1966).

Lodge Road Unitarian Church, W. Bromwich (1870-1995)

Concert programmes, handbills etc.

Smethwick Musical Society (1900-17)

WILTSHIRE

Wiltshire and Swindon Record Office

Children's School Concert Programmes (1883-85)

Swindon College of Further Education

Swindon theatre and opera programmes (1932-39)

Warminster: Minster C.E. school (1903-40, miscellaneous)

WIRRAL

Wirral Archives Service

Irby Musical Society

Minutes of General Meetings (1945-52) with programmes and press cuttings.

WORCESTER

Worcester City Library

Programmes relating to Worcester, Malvern and Bromesgrove, including musical events held at Worcester Cathedral.

Worcester County Library

Three Choirs Festival

Festival concert programmes

Worcestershire Record Office

Sir Granville Bantock collection

*ca.*130 concert programmes (1893-1939)

Borough and Carpet Industry, etc.

Ranger-Keelaway duo concert programmes (1968)

Worcestershire Record Office (cont.)

Spencer Churchill (Northwick Park) Blockley, Glos.
*ca.*65 miscellaneous sale catalogues, concert programmes, circulars and other papers (*ca.*1830-40).

Leicester Family of Worcester
*ca.*65 copies of rules, concert programmes and other papers mainly relating to the Worcester Philharmonic Society (1878-86).

Sladden of Badsey
Concert programmes, press notices of concerts and operas, songs and other papers (1911-33).

YORK

York Minster Library

Grand Yorkshire Music Festival (1823-35)

YORKSHIRE

North Yorkshire County Record Office

Northallerton Grammar School (1910-11, 1924)

Tanfield choral society
Christmas concert programme (1925)

Papers of Francis Ernest Tombs
Concert programmes (1950)

West Yorkshire Archive Service, Bradford

Bradford City Tramways
Employees' concert, programme and word-book (1919)

Bradford concert programmes (1908-20, miscellaneous)

Bradford Fine Art and Industrial Exhibition, tickets (1882-1942)
Lister Park Promenade Concert programme (1942)

Bradford Gilbert and Sullivan Society records (1948-98)
Performance programmes (1950-97)
Concert programmes, with Brighouse and Rastrick Band (1977-95)

West Yorkshire Archive Service, Bradford (cont.)

Bradford Old Choral Society
Concert programmes (1906-29)

Bradford Subscription Concert programmes and papers of Jack Holgate (1865-1977)

St. Georges Hall, Bradford
Subscription concert programmes (1866-1909)

West Yorkshire Archive Service, Calderdale

W. H. Gledhill, printers of Elland, records
Collection of examples of work, including concert programmes.

West Yorkshire Archive Service, Kirklees

Dewsbury and District Music Society
Concert programmes (1950-54)

Huddersfield and Holmfirth
Concert programmes for choirs and brass bands (1961-75)

Skelmanthorpe Feast Sing and Musical Festival (1906-72)

West Yorkshire Archive Service, Leeds

Churwell Junior and Infant School
Concert programmes of Churwell Board Schools (1882-92)

Leeds concert programmes (1945-55)
Miscellaneous collection, acquired 1999 (accession no. 4386)

Appendix 2

Concert Programmes held by the British Library

The following list gives brief descriptions and shelfmarks of major collections of programmes held by the British Library. Individually catalogued programmes, of which the library has *ca.* 7000, are not listed here. For a more detailed listing, see the *Catalogue of Printed Music in the British Library to 1980* (vol.46) and the *General Catalogue of Printed Books*. The library also has a substantial collection of playbills, with programmes of musical performances interspersed with theatre performances. The coverage extends to theatres throughout the UK. A register by location is given in *British Museum Register of Playbills, Programmes and Theatre Cuttings* (typescript, shelfmark X.985/531).

Aldeburgh

Aldeburgh Festival (1948-, wanting 1950-52) P.P.2495.dal.

Arányi Collection

A collection of papers of the two British violinist sisters of Hungarian origin, Adila Adrienne Adalbertina Maria Fachiri, née d'Arányi and Jelly Eva d'Arányi de Hunyadvar, including programmes, press cuttings, letters, contracts, 1906-56.
Music Misc. Aranyi

Ayrton Papers

Beethoven Quartett Society (1845-46)
Queen Square Concerts (1832, 1834),
Queen Square Select Society (1844-45) Add. 52347

Baines Manuscripts

Programmes of recitals by William Baines and others, of his music (1915-56).
Add. 50235

Bath

Bath and Somersetshire 1st Triennial Grand Musical Festival (1824)
Programmes and word-books with MS notes by Sir George Smart.
Case 61.g.2.

Bedfont

Programmes and word-books of concerts given at Bedfont (1864-84)
f.756.(1.)

Berlin

Barth'sche Madrigal-Vereinigung
Programmes of 7 concerts (1903-05, 1911-13) g.1763.(2.)

Concertdirection Hermann Wolff
Berlin Philharmonic Orchestra: 5 concerts conducted by Hans von Bülow and Richard Strauss (1891-95), programmes. 1560/1472.

Hochschule für Musik (1878-79) g.1763.(3.)

Kaiser-Wilhelm-Gedächtnis-Kirche (1962-) X.0439/13

Birmingham

Birmingham Musical Association 7879.t.34.
Saturday Evening Popular Concerts in the Town Hall (1879-81)
Concerts 4, 6, 7, 8, 11, 13, 14, 15, 22, 45, with MS notes.

Chappell Society for the Relief of Aged and Distressed Housekeepers
15 concerts given at St. Paul's Chapel and in the Town Hall (1829-36).
7897.d.34.

Programme for 2 Jan 1828 RB.23.b.3782.(20.)

City of Birmingham Symphony Orchestra
1920-21 7887.b.42.
1953-78 Cup.918/17

Harmonic Society (1829) 7898.m.13.(4.)

Masonic Hall (1875-94, with MS notes) 7895.s.15.

Private Concerts (1829-34) 7897.d.33.

Town Hall 7902.e.16.
Mr. Halford's Orchestral Concerts (1897-1901, 100 programmes)

Triennial Festival (Birmingham Musical Festival)
Programmes and word-books (1823-1909); wanting the programmes for 1846, 1864, and 1906; no Festival held between 1829 and 1834. A number of programmes contain the autographs of composers and performers associated with the Festival. 7894.s.1.

Boult Papers

Advertisements and programmes for concerts probably attended by Sir Adrian Boult (1895-1977) Add. 72675-76

Programmes, posters and details of subscriptions for concerts for which Boult was a performer or conductor (1896-1977) Add. 72677-78

Bournemouth

Bournemouth Symphony Orchestra and Bournemouth Sinfonietta: concert programmes and seasonal programmes (1954-78) Cup.918/15

Breslau

Bohn'scher Gesangverein (1894-1909) d.486

Brighton

Royal Pavilion

2nd Brighton Music Festival (1910, concerts 1-5) X.431/435.

Programmes of concerts held in the Dome L.23.c.10.(13.)

Programmes of 20 concerts held in the Dome (1870-77) 1572/208.

Bristol

Bristol Madrigal Society

4 programmes (13 Jan, 4, 11 Nov 1916, 21 Jan 1920) 7897.m.21.

Bristol Musical Festival

7 programmes (12th Festival, 1908) X.431/433.

Programmes and word-book, with a prospectus and booklet containing portraits of performers (13th Festival, 1912) X.431/423.

Grand Musical Festival Case

Programmes and word-books of 6 concerts (1814) 61.g.4.

British Music Manuscripts

Programmes of concerts given under the direction of Dr H. Watson (6 Feb 1906, 20 March 1907, and 24 March 1909) Add. 50781 D

Buckhurst Hill

Programmes of concerts given under the direction of J.O. Marshall (1907-08) d.488.j.(10.)

Bury St. Edmund's

Grand Musical Festival (1828)
With MS notes by Sir George Smart. Case 61.g.5.

Cambridge

Cambridge Grand Musical Festival (1833)
With MS notes by Sir George Smart. Case 61.g.6.

Collection (1835) Case 61.g.19.
With MS notes by Sir George Smart, including a concert marking the installation of the Marquis Camden as Chancellor of the University.

Concerts given at Cambridge (1875-78) f.757.

Cambridge University Musical Society
Programmes and word-books of the society's concerts (miscellaneous) and of the Tuesday and Wednesday popular concerts (1862-1978). d.489.

Cardiff

Cardiff Triennial Musical Festival
Prospectus and 8 programmes (1902) X.431/425.
8 programmes (1904) X.431/424.
8 programmes and word-books (1907) e.1391.a.

Chagrin Papers

Papers of the composer, conductor and administrator Francis Chagrin, including concert programmes (1927-74). MSS Mus. *2-83*.

Chapel Hill 7901.e.19.

University of North Carolina, Department of Music (1952-53, 1957-58)

Ernest Chapman Papers

Papers of Ernest Chapman relating to the journal *Tempo*, and to the Macnaghten Concerts (1939-73) Add. 62948-52

Ernest Chapman Papers (cont.)

Publicity brochures, concert programmes, etc., relating to Ernest Chapman as concert manager of the electronic music group *Intermodulation* (1970, 1971)
Add. 64956

Cologne

Programme of the *Grande Fête Musicale,* Cologne (7, 8 June 1835), directed by Felix Mendelssohn-Bartholdy. Add. 33507, fol.242

Curzon Collection

Printed notes on various works, mostly extracted from programmes of concerts given by Clifford Curzon (1958, n.d) Add. 65084

Darnton Collection

Programmes for the Adolph Hallis Chamber Music Concerts and for performances of Darnton's works (1934-76) Add. 62773 B

Norman Del Mar Collection

Miscellaneous papers relating to Strauss MS Mus. 121

Programmes for the Richard Strauss Festival (St. James's Hall, London, 1903), *Elektra* (Covent Garden, 1910), 2 concerts conducted by Sir Thomas Beecham (Theatre Royal, 1947), *Die Ägyptische Helena* (Munich, 1956) and *Die Schweigsame Frau* (Bühnen der Stadt Essen, 1961 and Covent Garden, 1961).

Derby

Derby Musical Festival (1831)
With MS notes by Sir George Smart Case 61.g.7.

Ernö Dohnányi Manuscripts

Concert programmes (1899-1957) Add. 50807

Dohnányi Supplementary Collections

Concert programmes (1904-31, 1960) Add. 51067

Dublin

1st Dublin Grand Musical Festival (1831, 6 concerts)
With MS notes by Sir George Smart. Case 61.g.8.

Edinburgh

Edinburgh Grand Musical Festival (1819 and 1824)
With MS notes by Sir George Smart. Case 61.g.9.

International Festival of Music and Drama
Miscellaneous programmes of events (1951-) 07903.e.25.

Usher Hall (1939-) W.P.13132.

Feltham

Miscellaneous concerts (1867-83) f.756.(2.)

'Fragmenta'

A collection of parts of books, cuttings from newspapers, advertisements, play-bills, etc. made by Francis Cox (94 vols.,1788-1833). MS list by Cecil B. Oldman given in *British Museum Register of Playbills, Programmes and Theatre Cuttings* (shelfmark X.985/531). 937.g.1-94.

Frankfurt am Main

Miscellaneous concerts (1873 and 1874) f.755

Glasgow

Glasgow Choral Union (1877-94)
Scottish Orchestral Company (1893-94)
Glasgow Choral and Orchestral Union (1894-99) d.491.

Scottish Orchestra Company
13 Classical Orchestral Concerts programmes, St. Andrew's Hall, Glasgow (1893-94), with a prospectus of the company. 7901.aa.42.

Gloucester

Gloucester Musical Festival

1853	7896.h.43.(3.)
1871, 1874, 1877	7899.d.1.
1874-1947 (48 concerts)	7903.bb.3.
1889 (166th Meeting of the Three Choirs)	7897.d.32.(3.)
1892	7899.dd.3.

Great Britain

Arts Council of Great Britain 7900.p.8.

8 concerts of Henry Purcell's music. Commemorative book of programmes, notes and texts, with essays by Denis Arundell, Watkins Shaw, and others (London, 1951).

British Broadcasting Corporation

BBC Chamber Music concerts (1932-) W.P.11199.
BBC Light Programme concerts (1946-) W.P.15508.
BBC Concert Orchestra concerts (1955-) 7902.n.3.

Federation of British Music Industries

6th, 8th and 9th Summer Courses in Music Teaching, London (1927, 1929-30) 7897.w.35.

Gregynog

Programmes of concerts and music festivals held at Gregynog.
Newtown, Montgomeryshire, Gregynog Press (1924-33) C.102.f.3.

Halifax

Halifax Grand Musical Festival 10347.ee.14.(7.)

3 programmes and word-books (29, 30 Sept and 1 Oct 1830)

Hamburg

Conventgarten

Programmes of 68 orchestral and instrumental concerts held principally at the Concerthaus of the Conventgarten (1886-94) 1608/3137

Haslemere

Haslemere Festival of Chamber Music

Programme (1931) Hirsch 1243.(2.)
Festival programmes, with MS notes (1961-) X.435/912.
Festival programmes (1964-) P.431/35.

Hereford

Hereford Music Meeting

1822 (96th Meeting of the Three Choirs) 1870.d.1.(117.)
1837 (programme and 5 word-books) 7899.ee.5.(11.)
1870-1949 (65 programmes and word-books) 7903.bb.1.
1885 (162nd Meeting of the Three Choirs) 7897.d.32.(2.)
1906 (programme and 7 word-books) c.376

Myra Hess Cuttings

Press cuttings relating to the pianist Dame Myra Hess (1901-65). Also included are related printed and typewritten papers, including several concert programmes. Add. 59859-61

Hollander Papers

Miscellaneous papers and personal correspondence, including concert programmes, press reviews, etc.(1896-1936) Add. 53767

Hovingham

10th Musical Festival at Hovingham Hall (1900) f.761.(1.)

Hull

Kingston-upon-Hull Grand Musical Festival (1834, 1840)
With MS notes by Sir George Smart Case 61.g.11

Arthur Hutchings Collection

Papers of the musicologist Arthur Hutchings, including concert programmes (1922-50). MSS Mus. 86.

International Musical Society

4th Congress of the International Musical Society (London, 1911)
General programme and 3 other programmes 7897.m.24

International Society for Contemporary Music

Miscellaneous concert programmes (1937-) X.435/1007

Prospectuses, programmes and proceedings of festivals and congresses organised by the Society (1923-48). Another set of programmes at Hirsch 1492.
7889.d.11.

Leeds

City Council Libraries and Arts Committee Cup.918/21
Programmes of individual concerts held under the auspices of the City of Leeds Libraries and Arts Committee, and seasonal programmes (1956-78).

Leeds Musical Festival

1880, 1883, 1886, 1889, 1892, 1898, 1913	D-07899.i.22.
1883	R.M.5.d.9.
1886	7897.l
1953, 1964, 1967, 1970, 1972, 1974, 1976	Cup.918/19

Leicester

Leicester Orchestral Union (1879-1921) P.901/25.

Leningrad

Gosudarstvennaia Akademicheskaia Filarmoniia
81 programmes (1927-28) 7888.e.9.

Liverpool

Liverpool Grand Musical Festival Case 61.g.12
With MS notes by Sir George Smart (1823, 1827, 1830, 1833, 1836)

Liverpool Philharmonic Society
1900-08 RB.23.a.1568
1864-66, 1871-79, 1892-99, 1910-14, 1931-32 P.431/75.
1950-78 Cup.918/18

Llandudno

Llandudno Pier Co.
Concert programmes (1928-) W.P.15062.

London

Æolian Hall I.600.c.(225.)
5 historical cello recitals by Boris Hambourg (1906)
Programmes for 23 concerts given in the Æolian Hall, including the 1923 and 1924 series of Goossens Chamber Concerts X.0435/117.

Alexandra Palace (1875-77, 40 items) 7901.aa.44.

Prisoners of War Camp: Konzertverein
Programmes of orchestral and other concerts given in the camp (1916-18; 146 programmes) X.431/754.

Amateur Concerts (1818-22)
With MS notes by Sir George Smart Case 61.h.2.(1.)

Amateur Musical Society
An album containings a prospectus of the Society, rules, lists of members, statements of accounts, concert programmes for the 1st to 14th season (1847-60) K.6.c.1.

London (cont.)

The Bach Choir (1876-) e.1400
Wanting the programmes for concerts 3, 6-9, 11, 13, 14 and 16.

Walter Bache's Concerts
Programmes, MS and printed, of piano recitals and concerts given in London by Walter Bache (1865-88) 7897.e.39.

Ballet Club Theatre (1935-) X.435/1006.

Bechstein Hall
Concert Club programmes (1905-08) X.439/521

Beecham Sunday Concerts (1934-35)
Concerts at the Queen's Hall X.439/12016.

Beethoven Quartett Society (1845) d.54

Begin. People's Subscription Band
13 programmes of the music performed in Regent's Park on Sundays of the summer of 1857 D-7895.b.12.

The British Library
British Library Stefan Zweig series, Wigmore Hall (1987-97) YM.1988.b.286
Music in Context series, British Library Auditorium (2001-03)

British Orchestral Society (1872-75) c.372.

Broadwood Concerts (1902-12) 7898.p.

J. Capell Private Concerts (1817-21, 1824-28)
With MS notes by Sir George Smart Case 61.h.4.(2.)

Choral Harmonists (1838-50) 7899.d.4.

Civil Service Musical Society (1864-80) 7899.bb.4.

Civic and Municipal Institutions: Livery Companies
Music at the banquets of various Livery Companies (1879-80)
7897.m.8.

London (cont.)

Concerts of Ancient Music

New Rooms, Tottenham Street, London.

Programmes (1780-1847) 11784.e.1.
Wanting the vols. for 1783, 1785, 1787-94, 1799, 1813, 1824, 1832.

Word-books (1782-1848) 54.b.1-15. & 11778.a
Wanting the vols. for 1783 and 1811

Programmes (1782-1813) 54.b.1-15.
Wanting the vols. for 1783, 1789, 1791 and 1804-08.

Programmes (1789-1848) 11778.a.
Wanting the volumes for 1790, 1792, 97, 1799 and 1811.

Programmes (1793-1842) 11784.de.1.
Wanting the vol. for 1784.

Programmes (1805-08, 1810) 51.b.24-28.

Programmes of single concerts (1793, 1804, 1840-42)
R.M.5.a.1.

Programmes (1831-48) R.M.5.a.2.
Wanting the volumes for 1840 and 1847.

Covent Garden Theatre

Beecham Sunday Concerts (1936-39) d.479
Wanting programmes of concert 16 in the 1937-38 season, and concerts 1, 2, 7, 8 in the 1938-39 season.

Beecham Sunday Concerts (1936-37) P.431/290.
Wanting programmes for concerts 3, 4, 7, 8 and 10.

Covent Garden Theatre (1959-) P.7613.kl.

Covent Garden Theatrical Fund

Handbills, etc., relating to the annual dinners of the Covent Garden Theatrical Fund (1825-44), with MS letters and programmes of the music performed by Sir George Smart. C.61.i.2.

London (cont.)

Cripplegate Theatre (1959-, miscellaneous) W.P.16475.

Crosby Hall (1838-56) d.494.

Curtius Concert Club (1899-1900) b.622.

Arnold Dolmetsch Concerts (1892-1900) b.620.

English National Opera (1959-66) P.P.7613.kq.

Exeter Hall X.431/436.(1-4.)

Programmes of a performance of J.S. Bach's *St. Matthew Passion* on 6 April 1870 and of subscription concerts on 23 Jan and 6 Feb 1872.

Grand Festival of Sacred Music at Exeter Hall for the Charing Cross Hospital (April 1836). Programmes, word-books, etc., with MS notes by Sir George Smart. C.61.g.10.

Grand Festival of Sacred Music at Exeter Hall for the Charing Cross Hospital (1836). Programmes, word-books, etc., with MS notes by Sir George Smart. Case 61.g.10.

Wednesday evening concerts, 1-3 (1853) P.P.1948.bb.

Freemasons Hall

Handbills, etc., relating to the annual dinners in aid of the Covent Garden Theatrical Fund, with MS programmes of the music performed by Sir George Smart (1825-44) Case 61.i.2.

Friday Popular Concerts

Programme and analytical remarks for concert at the *Salle de Saint Jacques* on Friday Evening, 27 April 1894, by L. S. Benson and J. A. Fuller-Maitland, with MS notes. A parody of the programme books of the Popular Concerts at St. James's Hall. d.480.a.

Gloucester House

Programme of a concert at Gloucester House (30 June 1853) plus a collection of Buckingham Palace concert programmes (1837-60). Cup.403.w.6.

Grotrian Hall (1938-) X.800/33522.

London (cont.)

Highbury Philharmonic Society (1893 and 1897) d.488.a.(6.)

London Glee and Madrigal Union
Word-books of 7 concerts (1860) 11781.d.23.(5-11.)
Word-books and programmes of 3 concerts (1861) 11651.d.29.(10.)

Handel Society (1902-03) e.1403.a

Hanover Square Rooms
Queen's Concert Rooms, Hanover Square, 3rd season. Ernst Pauer's 3 Historical Performances of Pianoforte Music in strictly chronological order. Programmes of recitals on 27 Nov, 4 and 11 Dec 1867, with comments, critical remarks, and biographies. d.488.l.(1.)

Hawes's Concerts
Word-books of concerts given by Mr. Hawes (10, 12, 24 March 1830) 7899.ee.5.(2.)
Programmes, books of the words, etc., of the Annual Concerts given by W. Hawes (1818-19, 1824-39) and by W.& M. B. Hawes (1840-41). With MS notes by Sir George Smart, W. Hawes and M. B. Hawes Case 61.h.4.(3.)

Henschel Vocal Recitals
Programmes and 11 word-books for Mr and Mrs Henschel's Vocal Recitals (1889-92) c.374.a.(2.)

Lamoureux Concerts d.485.
Concerts given at Queen's Hall by Charles Lamoroureux (1896-98)

London Musical Festival, Queen's Hall (1899-1902, imperfect) e.1396.a
London International College, Spring Grove (1871-75) f.756.(3.)

London Subscription Concerts (1817-19) Case 61.h.2.(2.)
With MS notes by Sir George Smart

London Symphony Concerts (1886-97, imperfect) c.374

Lyceum Theatre
Promenade concert programmes (1838-40, imperfect) 7892.tt.12.
5 programmes for the season of Russian opera (1931) L.49/1223.

London (cont.)

Macnaghten Concerts HS.74/ X.0435/3

Concert programmes collected by Ernest Chapman, not catalogued separately (1931-80). With 2 boxes containing 10 unbound programmes and an index of composers.

Magpie Minstrels Madrigal Society (1888-1911) g.1760.

Mansion House

Programmes and word-books, letters, etc., relating to concerts given at the Mansion House and Guildhall (1817, 1820-22, 1828-30). With MS notes by Sir George Smart Case 61.i.3

Miscellaneous institutions

A collection of analytical programmes of concerts given at the Crystal Palace, St. James's Hall, the Royal Academy of Music and the Queen's Hall (1886-96). X.439/522

National Gallery Concerts

Miscellaneous programmes (1940-) X.439/11999.

A collection, made by Dame Myra Hess, of programmes and other material relating to the National Gallery Concerts (1939-46), including: daily programmes; (with MS notes of attendances and receipts); weekly programmes; catalogue of works performed (1939-44; 2 copies, compiled in MS by Harold Ferguson and others, one with MS additions for performances between 1944 and 1946); 2 card-index boxes, containing MS lists of performers and the dates of their performances; notebook listing, in MS, dates of first performances. Cup.404.c.1.
Cup.404.c.1/1.-11

New Musical Fund

Programmes, word-books, autograph letters, etc., relating to concerts given in aid of the New Musical Fund, with MS notes by Sir George Smart (1794, 1805, 1815-41) Case 61.g.20

New Philharmonic Society

Programme books of the 1st, 2nd, 3rd, 5th, & 6th concerts of the 1st season, and the 3rd, 4th, & 6th of the 2nd season. (1852-53) e.1395.a.(1.)

London (cont.)

Oratorio Concerts

Programmes of oratorio concerts, principally given at Drury Lane, Covent Garden, and the King's Theatres, with MS notes by Sir George Smart (1813-26). The programmes of 2 concerts at Cheltenham in 1818 are included.

Case 61.i.1

Philanthropic Society's Chapel (1825-29, 1831, 1833)

Word-books with MS notes by Sir George Smart Case 61.h.4.(1.)

Philharmonic Society (see also Royal Philharmonic Society)

Programmes (1813-68), with MS notes by Sir George Smart (wanting programmes for season 55 and all but one of the programmes for season 56).

K.6.d.3.

Programmes (1869-1912) e.1401

Quartett Concerts (1836-59, imperfect)

Collection of programmes and word-books, Hanover Square Rooms and Crosby Hall, with MS notes by F.G. Edwards. d.483.

Queen's Hall

Thomas Beecham Orchestral Concerts d.488.k.(1.)

Annotated programmes for concerts 1 and 2 (22 Feb, 15 March 1909)

Beethoven Festival

Professor J. Kruse's Beethoven Festival (May 1903)

8 programme-books e.1396.d.(1.)

Professor J. Kruse's 2nd Musical Festival (April 1904)

7 programme books e.1396.d.(2.)

British Chamber Music Concerts

10 programmes and word-books (1894-) d.484.

Colonne Orchestra (1896) d.488.b.(1.)

Mr. F. B. Ellis Modern Orchestral Music (1914) d.488.k.(2.)

Balfour Gardiner Choral and Orchestral Concerts

Concerts 1-4 (1913) e.1396.f.(2.)

London (cont.)

Queen's Hall (cont.)

London Ballad Concerts

3 word-books (Jan - March 1900) c.371.f.(1.)
8 word-books (1896-97, 1899) d.488.b.(4.)

London Symphony Orchestra

Programmes of 7 special symphony concerts (1919-20)
P.431/222.
Programmes of 17 concerts, third series (1906-07)
7903.c.28.

Miscellaneous concerts

16 word-books for:
Chaikovsky Concerts (15 June 1898, 14 June 1899)
Wagner Concerts (7 Nov 1898, 10 June, 13 Nov, 4 Dec 1899)
Ysaÿe Concerts (30 May, 12 June, 17 June 1899; 17 May, 31 May, 21 Nov 1900)
Miss Blauvelt's Concerts (4 July 1899, 27 June 1900)
Newman Testimonial Concert (13 Dec 1899)
Good Friday Concert (13 April 1900) d.484.c

8 concert programmes (1901-09) 11797.f.3.
16 analytical concert programmes (1898-1900) d.484.c.
40 concert programmes (1909-45) X.0431/534.
Miscellaneous concerts (1896-1904) e.1396.c

Nikisch Orchestral Concerts

4 analytical programmes (1895) e.1398.
Berlioz centenary (11 Dec 1903) e.1396.b.(2.)

(Henry Wood) Promenade Concerts

Programmes (1896-1909, 1911-17, 1919, 1921, 1923, 1926)
Wanting various programmes for 1903. h.5470

Programmes (1902, 1904)
Wanting programmes for 6, 26 Sept and 1 Oct 1902. h.5470.a

Programmes (1927-) W.P.193

Queen's Hall Choral Society (1895, etc.) e.1396

London (cont.)

Queen's Hall (cont.)

Queen's Hall Symphony Concerts (1897) d.484.a

Sunday Afternoon Orchestral Concerts

Analytical programmes of *Sunday Afternoon Orchestral Concerts*, afterwards *Sunday Afternoon Concerts* and subsequently concerts of the *Sunday Concert Society*, given at the Queen's Hall (1896-1907, imperfect).
d.484.d.

Sunday Evening Concerts and Sunday Evening Chamber Concerts

Analytical programmes of *Sunday Evening Concerts*, afterwards concerts of the *Sunday Concert Society*, given at the Queen's Hall (1898-99), with analytical notes by E. F. Jacques. d.484.e. - d.484.f

Wagner Concerts

23 programmes and word-books of Wagner concerts, conducted by Felix Mottl and others (1894-98) g.1761.a.

Royal Academy of Music

Programmes of students' orchestral concerts and students' chamber concerts (1891-94, imperfect). d.482.

Royal Albert Hall

3 analytical programmes (1874) e.1395.a.(3.)

Davidson's Musical Programmes

11 concert programmes (1871-79) e.1399.a.

Elgar Festival (1949)

11 concerts held mainly at the Royal Albert Hall and organised by the Henry Wood Concert Society. X.431/983

London International Exhibition (1873)

6 word-books d.488.l.(3.)

Madame Patti

Word-books of concerts at which Madame Patti sang (1889-94; 1896-99)
e.1399.(3.)
e.1399.c.(4.)

London (cont.)

Royal Albert Hall (cont.)

Miscellaneous programmes and word-books (1873-1901)
e.1399.c.

Promenade Concerts

See also Queen's Hall: (Henry Wood) Promenade Concerts

Programmes of Sir Henry Wood's Jubilee Season Promenade Concerts (June 1944) 7890.aa.7.

Scotch and Irish Concerts

Word-books (1894-98, 1901) e.1399.c.(3.)

Wagner Festival (1877)

5 programmes and word-books 7896.f.33

8 programmes and word-books 11746.k.11

Henry Wood Concert Society

Programmes of 52 concerts presented by the Henry Wood Concert Society (1946-69) X.431/981

Royal Choral Society

Word-books and programmes of concerts given by the Royal Choral Society (1891-) e.1399.b.

Royal College of Music

Patron's Fund concerts (1904-07) d.488.j.(1.)

Royal Festival Hall

Concert and recital programmes for the Royal Festival Hall, Queen Elizabeth Hall and Purcell Room (1957-) W.P.4462.

Royal Philharmonic Society (see also Philharmonic Society)

Programmes (1912-) e.1401

Programmes of 8 concerts of choral and orchestral music presented by the Royal Philharmonic Society in association with the Arts Council of Great Britain, the BBC and the London County Council to celebrate the coronation of Her Majesty Queen Elizabeth II (1953). e.1401.a

London (cont.)

Sacred Harmonic Society
Programmes and word-books (1837-81?) d.493.

South Place Sunday Concert Society
Sunday Popular Concerts (1931-) X.435/1008.

St. James's Hall
Monday Popular Concerts - Saturday Popular Concerts
Programme and words (7 Feb 1859-7 March 1904) d.480.
Wanting programmes for 1902/03, and various programmes for 1859-1864, 1867-1873, 1877-78, 1901-02, and 1903-04.
Saturday Popular Concerts (1873-86) 7902.b.40.

Mr. Charles Halle's Beethoven Recitals
Programmes for the 8 recitals (1862) 7901.aa.4

Miscellaneous
13 programmes of miscellaneous concerts and recitals given by Mr. G. Grossmith, Mdlle. Chaminade, M. Paderewski, Mr. Barrington Toote, the Bristol Royal Orpheus Glee Society, Madame A. Svetloffsky, Mdlle. Landi and Miss M. V. White (1889-96). d.487

20 programmes and word-books (1883-91) c.371.(3.)
13 programmes and word-books (1883-1904) e.1397.b.
13 programmes and word-books (1889-96) d.487.
4 programmes and word-books (1892-94) c.371.b.(3.)
5 programmes and word-books (1892-94) e.1402.a.(2.)
8 programmes and word-books of various concerts given at St. James's Hall and Queen's Hall (1893-96) d.488.
9 programmes and word-books (1893-98) d.488.d.(2.)
5 programmes and word-books (1894-96) c.371.d.
9 programmes and word-books of St. James's Hall Ballad Concerts (1894-99) e.1397.
6 programmes and word-books (1895-99) d.488.c.(3.)
6 programmes and word-books of concerts given by Plunket Greene and Leonard Borwick (1896-98) c.371.c.(4.)
7 programmes and word-books (1897-1900) d.487.a.
8 programmes and word-books (1898-1900) b.623.
6 programmes and word-books (1898-1904) b.623.a.
17 programmes and word-books (1899-1904) e.1397.a.(2.)

London (cont.)

St. James's Hall (cont.)

3 programmes and word-books (1901) c.371.g.(2.)

32 word-books (1873-91) c.371.

National Society for the Prevention of Cruelty to Children

Programme of a concert on Friday 13 June 1890 in Aid of the Funds of the National Society for the Prevention of Cruelty to Children. d.487.c.(1.)

Novello's Oratorio Concerts

13 programmes and word-books (1885-89) X.431/431.

Oratorio Concerts

Programmes of 26 *Oratorio Concerts*, mostly with word-books, given between 23 May 1867 and 6 Feb 1872, and conducted by Sir Joseph Barnby. With prospectuses of the 2nd and 3rd seasons. X.431/436.(1-4.)

Richter Concerts

Concerts conducted by Hans Richter (24, 31 May, 3, 7, 10, 11 June 1880; 24 Oct 1881; 3, 8 May, 5, 9 June 1882; and summer season 1890-95) X.439/1271

Programmes of the Orchestral Festival and the Richter Concerts (1879-1904) d.481.

Richard Strauss Festival

6 programme books (3-9 June 1903) d.487.b

Symphony Concerts

Programmes for the concerts 1, 5 and 6 in the 4th Season (1 May, 15 June, 22 June 1882), with analytical remarks by George Grove. d.488.l.(6.)

Donald Francis Tovey's Concerts of Chamber Music

Concerts 1-4 (Nov 1900) d.490.

St. Martin's Town Hall

2 word-books of concerts by the Amsterdam a Cappella Choir and by Miss Holland's Choir (1894). c.371.b.(4.)

Stock Exchange Orchestral Society

Concerts on 19 Dec 1894, 3 Dec 1895, 8 Dec 1896, and 5 Dec 1898, at the Queen's Hall. d.488.b.(5.)

London (cont.)

Victoria and Albert Museum

Programmes of concerts held at the Museum (1952-) W.P.A.516.

Westminster Abbey

Royal Musical Festival (1834) Case 61.g.17

With MS notes by Sir George Smart

Willis's Rooms

Programmes for Ernst Pauer's 6 Historical Performances of Pianoforte Music (April-June 1863). 7895.bb.24.

10 programmes of Harrison and Knyvett's Vocal Concerts (1793) 1508/565.(1.)

Prospectus, programmes and word-books of 6 concerts given by Mrs. Billington, J. Braham and G. Naldi, with MS notes by Sir George Smart (1810). Case 61.g.18

Henry Wood Concert Society

79 programmes and word-books of concerts sponsored by the Henry Wood Concert Society (1946-69). Many programmes bear the autograph signatures of conductors and performers. X.431/981.

11 programmes of concerts sponsored by the Henry Wood Concert Society for the Elgar Festival (30 May-15 June 1949). Many programmes bear the autograph signatures of conductors and performers. X.431/983.

Young People's Orchestral Concerts

Analytical programmes, by J. Bennett, of 3 concerts conducted by G. Henschel (1890). c.374.a.(1.)

Lucas Collection

Scrapbook containing concert programmes and press cuttings relating to performances of works by Mary Anderson Lucas, apparently assembled by the composer (1923-51). Add. 69812

Alick Maclean Collection

Concert programmes (1880-1960), including programmes of organ recitals by Quentin Maclean. MS Mus. 203

Manchester

Hallé Concerts Society
Programmes for the 1898-99 season (20 concerts). 1560/657

Jubilee Concert programme (30 Jan 1908) X.419/1593

Programmes of individual concerts given by the Hallé Orchestra, and seasonal programmes (1952-78) Cup.918/16

Manchester Grand Musical Festival (1836) Case 61.g.13
Programmes, word-books, with MS notes by Sir George Smart

Manchester Opera House
Programmes, etc. (1932-) P.P.5224.egb.

Melbourne

Mr. Joseph Gillott's Concerts
Annotated programmes, 2nd edition (1887) 7898.c.8.(5.)

Mebourne Philharmonic Society (1859-68) 7895.ee.5.

Mendelssohn-Bartholdy, Felix

Draft programmes for concerts at the Leipzig Gewandhaus, 1 January to 23 March 1843. Add. 33965

Miscellaneous collections

Programmes of concerts given in London, Leicester, Dublin, Glasgow, Edinburgh, Blackheath, Ryde and Sydenham (1834-59) 7897.i.24.(29.)

A collection of programmes of oratorio concerts, principally given at Drury Lane, Covent Garden, and the King's Theatres (1813-26). With MS notes by Sir George Smart Case 61.i.1

Programmes, word-books, and MS accounts relating to concerts and operas given at Bath, Bristol and Cheltenham (1818-46). With MS notes by Sir George Smart Case 61.g.1

A collection of playbills and concert programmes, English and foreign, chiefly of the London Theatres (1836-46) Playbills 300

Programmes, posters, etc., of concerts, oratorios given in London (1816-65)
Playbills 320

French, German and Italian concert, opera, theatre programmes and similar material (1936-63, 31 items). X.431/2098.

Programmes of concerts of music conducted by Sir Henry Wood (1898-1944). Many programmes bear MS inscriptions by Sir Henry Wood and others.
X.435/115.

Concert programmes, orders of service, and other works, mostly in honour of Sir Henry J. Wood (1893-1969, 25 items) X.435/116.

English ballet, concert, opera and theatre programmes and similar material (1932-74). Collected by Diana Gordon X.435/318.

Programmes of music performed at Worcester College, Oxford; Dover College and elsewhere; with other matter. Collected by A. H. Stevens, (1878?-1921?)
7900.f.41.

Programmes of concert, opera and theatre performances given in Berlin and other European cities (1917-34). Collected by Lily Marian Rosenberg.
C.186.d.1

Miscellaneous concert programmes formed by Sir W. S. Gilbert (1891-93, 39 items).
Th.Cts.78.(13.)

9 miscellaneous London concerts (1879-90) e.1402

Miscellaneous concert and opera programmes (1926-) X.0435/4.

Programmes of concerts given at Hanworth, Isleworth, Kew and Richmond, 1871-84.
f.756.(4.)

Programmes of concerts in Germany (1892-1938) and England (1938-66). Collected by Ernst Henschel Henschel

Collection formed by William Edmonds (1888-1913) Cup.1247.ccc.5.

Miscellaneous Letters of Musicians MS Mus. 133 A-J.
Signed concert programmes (1941-3, n.d.)

Miscellaneous collections (cont.)

Programmes for 2 concerts by the Hallé Orchestra in Rochdale and a piano recital by Pouishnoff, with a sheet bearing further signatures.
Miscellaneous concert programmes (1899-1933)

Miscellaneous collection of programmes of concerts given principally in London from 1860 to 1925, initiated by William Barclay Squire (*ca.* 8000 items). Venues include Prince's Hall, Piccadilly, Collard's Concert Rooms, Steinway Hall, Edward Dannreuther's house and the Meistersingers' Club.
7892.w.1

Collection of programmes of concerts given in Berlin, Paris and elsewhere on the continent 748.e.10

Collection of programmes of concerts, musical festivals given in the provinces
Cup.645.b.9

Konzert-Programm-Austausch, Jahrgang 8-21
A chronological series of programmes and word-books of European concerts, chiefly German. The programmes contained in each number are arranged alphabetically according to the place of performance. Leipzig, Breitkopf & Hartel (1901-14, wanting many numbers) P.P.1946.ad

Mozart, Wolfgang Amadeus

Programmes of Mozart operas and other classical music performed in chronological order at 45 Seymour Street and 20 Hans Road, London (1894-1913)
7888.a.62

Munich

Richard Strauss Woche (23-28 June 1910)
Programmes for 3 Festaufführungen in the Prinzregentheater, 3 Festkonzerte in the Neue Musik-Festhalle and 2 Morgen-Konzerte in the Münchener Künstlertheater. 7897.i.49

Nashville

University of Nashville, Peabody College
Division of Music Programmes (1945-47) Ac.2691.pa.

New York

Brighton Beach Music Hall 1600/830
Brighton Beach, New York (6 July 1889–29 Aug 1891)

New York (cont.)

Kurt Schindler

Programmes for 3 song recitals and a concert of Madrigals of the French Renaissance presented by Kurt Schindler (1908-10). Also includes programmes for 3 concerts of 'Musique vocale ancienne et moderne' arranged by Charles Gilibert. f.761.b.(2, 3.)

New York Pro Musica Antiqua

Programmes of concerts (1954-) 7902.g.27.

New York Schola Cantorum

Programmes of concerts (1922-) W.P.7501.

Newcastle-upon-Tyne

Newcastle-upon-Tyne Musical Festival

6 programmes and word-books (1909) e.1388

3 programmes (Oct 1909) X.431/434

Northumberland, Durham and Newcastle-upon-Tyne Grand Musical Festival

Programmes and word-books of the Festivals of 1824 and 1842 with MS notes by Sir George Smart. Case 61.g.14

Northern Sinfonia Orchestra

Programmes of individual concerts given by the Northern Sinfonia and seasonal programmes (1961-77) Cup.918/14

Norwich

Norwich Grand Musical Festival

3 programmes and word-books (Sept 1788) 7898.bb.10.(1.)

3 programmes and word-books (Sept 1790) 7898.bb.10.(2, 3.)

Programmes, word-books, etc. of the Festivals for 1824, 1827, 1830, 1833 and 1836 with MS notes by Sir George Smart Case 61.g.16

Norfolk and Norwich Triennial Musical Festival

Programmes, General Arrangements and word-books:

3rd Festival (1890) 7897.l.26

13th Festival (1860) 7896.h.44

24th Festival (1893) c.371.b.(6.)

25th Festival (1896) 7896.d.34

29th Festival (1908) e.1389.(2.)

Nottingham

St. Mary's Church P.P.2495.dai

Programmes of musical recitals and concerts (1955 etc.)

University of Nottingham

Programmes of plays, concerts and recitals given in the Great Hall of the University (1854) Ac.2673.b/13

University of Nottingham Music Society (1956-) W.P.12222.

O'Neill Papers

Papers of Norman O'Neill, composer, and of Adine O'Neill (née Rückert), pianist and teacher. The collection includes lecture recital programmes (1895-1942) Deposit 1999/04

Oxford

Music Room

Mr. Marshall's Concert (24 Feb 1834) 1879.c.1.(19.)

Concert programme (25 March 1776) I.600.c.(114.)

University Musical Festival

Word-books of Crotch's oratorio *The Captivity of Judah* and 3 miscellaneous concerts (1834) 7898.m.13.(12.)

Philadelphia

Free Library

Curtis String Quartet concert programmes (1948-) 7900.l.5.

Pittsfield, Massachusetts

Berkshire Festival of Chamber Music (1918-38) 7893.t.15.

Reading

Berkshire Grand Musical Festival

Programmes and word-books of the Festivals in 1819, 1822 and 1831, with MS notes by Sir George Smart. Case 61.g.3.

Henry Edward Rensburg Manuscripts

Concert programmes (1888-1927) MS Mus. 308

Rensburg was chairman of the Liverpool Arts Society and the Liverpool Philharmonic Orchestra, and music critic for the *Liverpool Daily Post*.

Ruhleben

Englaenderlager für Zivilgefangene, Ruhleben

Concert, theatre and sports programmes, educational prospectuses, newsletters and other documents produced by, and for, the prisoners of Ruhleben Concentration Camp (1914-18). Cup.900.tt.22.

San Francisco

Campion Society

Annual Campion Festival, 6th season onwards (1951-) W.P.C.191.

Humphrey Searle Collection

Programmes of concerts which included performances of Searle's own compositions and arrangements (1936-82) Add. 71832-33

Shanghai

Shanghai Municipal Orchestra (1923-24) X.431/56.

Sheffield

Sheffield Musical Festival

6 analytical programmes (1902) e.1393

Word-book (16 Oct 1800) 10347.f.6

6 programmes with analytical notes (1908) X.431/426

Victoria Hall

141 programmes of Mr. John Parr's Chamber Concerts, given at, Sheffield from 1 March 1930 to 2 May, 1957. e.1404.(2.)

Smart Papers

Correspondence and papers, including programmes and accompaniments (partly printed), relating to royal concerts and ceremonials (1819-66), and to the annual Festival of the Sons of the Clergy (1832-45). Add. 41777

A collection of printed programmes made by Sir George Smart during his European tour, July to December 1825. Add. 41775

List of London and Provincial Festivals and Concerts in which Sir George Smart was interested, either as conductor or composer, from 1798 to 1855, with directions for finding the programmes, with a view to bequeathing them to the British Museum. Add. 34278

Strachey Papers

Miscellaneous family papers, including copies of the wills of Lady Strachey and Philippa Strachey, family lists and bills, degree certificates, sketches, photographs and concert programmes. Add. 60653

Surbiton

Assembly Rooms 7901.cc.1

Mr. Joseph Ivimey's Chamber Concerts (1889-90, 1902-03)

Sydenham

Crystal Palace

Great Triennial Handel Festival

Programme of arrangements (1862) 7895.b.41.(3.)

Programme of arrangements (1865) 7895.b.41.(4.)

Programme of arrangements (1868) 7895.b.41.(5.)

Programme and word-book (1880) 7896.d.35 and 7899.d.2

Programme and word-book (1883) 7896.d.42

Programme and word-book (1885) 7895.e.28

Programme of arrangements (1885) 7898.c.8.(4.)

Programme and word-book (1888) 7896.d.43

Programmes and word-books for Festivals 1, 4, 6, 10 (1859-91) 7896.d.31

Saturday concerts (1867-1904, imperfect) c.370

Sunday School Centenary Festival (1880) B.512.s.(11.)

Sydney

University of Sydney

Programmes of music played on the War Memorial (1933) D-07899.i.14.

Carillon Music: 95 programmes and other documents (1928-33) D-07899.i.20.

Venice

Hospital of the Mendicanti

List of the performances of sacred music to be given by the pupils of the School of Music at the Mendicanti (1782) I.600.a.(162.)

Wandering Minstrels

Records of *The Wandering Minstrels*, a musical society which gave charity concerts in various places from 1860 to 1898. The collection includes programmes, press-cuttings, portraits, miscellaneous prints and drawings, musical manuscripts and a set of badges and buttons as worn by members of the Society. K.6.e.1-7

Washington, D.C.

Smithsonian Institution National Gallery of Art

Catalogues of exhibitions, concert programmes and other miscellaneous publications (1841) Ac.1875.ea.

Fred. E. Weatherly Collection

Miscellaneous papers, including occasional poems, concert programmes and memorial tributes (*ca.*1900-29) MS Mus. 115

Weil Papers

Collection of papers, entitled 'Siege of Mafeking: General Orders by Col. R. S. S. Baden-Powell.' Includes printed passes, vouchers, paper currency, programmes of concerts, etc. Add. 46851

Weimar

Programmes and libretti of *Fest-cantatas*, Weimar (1821-32)
Add. 32238

Worcester

Worcester Musical Festival

2 programmes and word-books (1842) 7895.b.50

Worcester Music meeting

9 programmes and word-books (1800-24) 1609/5766.

6 word-books of concerts (161st Meeting of the Three Choirs, 1884)
7897.d.(32.)

Worcester, Massachusetts

Worcester County Musical Association d.488.g.(6.)

Programmes of concerts in the 22nd Annual Festival (1879)

York

2nd Yorkshire Musical Festival (1825) 10347.ee.13.(8.)

4th Yorkshire Grand Musical Festival (1835) 7897.d.41
Word-books, York Minster (8-11 Sept) 10347.ee.13.(10.)

Wesley family

Register of juvenile concerts given by the brothers Charles and Samuel Wesley (1779-85), including lists of subscribers and, in the case of the last 4 series of concerts, also lists of those present, programmes, and accounts of expenses. Copied by Eliza Wesley in 1894 from the original belonging to Matthias Erasmus Wesley. Add. 35017

Frank Whitaker Papers Add. 51023 C

Programmes of BBC concerts on 7 Dec 1926 and 4 March 1929.

Wood Papers

Correspondence and papers of Sir Henry Wood and Lady Jessie Wood (1865-1971), including Wood's annotated copy of the prospectus for the 46th Season of Promenade Concerts (1940). Add. 56419-43

Appendix 3
Concert programmes held by the National Libraries of Scotland and Ireland

National Library of Scotland

Concert programmes listed in the library's online catalogue. The library also has a large collection of uncatalogued programmes, not listed here.

Balfour Handel Collection

Programmes relating to performances of music by Handel, gathered by Julian Marshall and purchased by the Library from the estate of its late owner, the Earl of Balfour, in 1937.

British Broadcasting Corporation

BBC Concert Orchestra

Miscellaneous prospectuses, programmes (1955-65) 6.1498

BBC Symphony Orchestra

Programmes (1930-) P.med.3629
P.sm.1166

Henry Wood Promenade Concerts

Programmes (1931-42) P.sm.1726
Programmes (1946-) P.med.3956
(lacking 1981-83, 1986-88, 1991-92.) P.sm.1726

Edinburgh

Edinburgh classical concerts

Festival performances of selected works by Beethoven at the Music Hall, Edinburgh (1912-13) NE.11.g.5(4-8)

Edinburgh International Festival

Programmes (1947-, lacking 1992) HP.la.1736
P.la.3998
P.med.1977

Edinburgh Musical Festival

Miscellaneous concert programmes (1819) 3.963(5)
3.1787(3)

Edinburgh (cont.)

Edinburgh Polish Song and Dance Ensemble
10th anniversary concert programme (1977) HP3.79.1173

French connections: Scotland and the arts of France
Leaflets produced to accompany the exhibition at the Edinburgh Royal Scottish Museum (1985) with concert programmes. GEB-I.1

Queen's Hall
Diaries of events (1982-94, incomplete) HP.med.767 PER
Programme of events (1994-) HP.med.767 PER

Glasgow

Choral and Orchestral Union of Glasgow H4.84.917
Programmes (1927-50, incomplete) HP1.78.4339

Empire Exhibition, Glasgow
Concert hall programmes (May-October 1938) NE.5.b.11

Glasgow Choral Union
Concert programmes (1866-80) Birk.87-91
Miscellaneous concert programmes (1882-83) NE.13.b.24

Glasgow Saturday afternoon musical recitals
Season 1907-08. EL.1.91.126

University of Glasgow
Department of Music concerts (1986-) HJ8.2136

Papers of William Hean Findlay

Collection of mostly concert programmes featuring Mr. J. Scott Skinner, the composer and fiddle player (1914-33). Some also featuring W. Hean Findlay. HP4.98.1407

Gregynog Press

Collection of ephemera printed at the Gregynog Press (Newtown, Montgomeryshire), including concert programmes, orders of service, and prospectuses (1926-62) FB.l.120(1-31)

Hopkinson Berlioz Collection

Programmes relating to performances of music by Berlioz, collected by Cecil Hopkinson, and presented to the Library in 1952.

Hopkinson Verdi Collection

Programmes relating to performances of music by Verdi, collected by Cecil Hopkinson, and purchased by the Library in 1970.

James Scott Hunter

Album of concert programmes, photographs and newspaper cuttings, many relating to James Scott Hunter (1909-41). H8.93.443

Malcolm MacFarlane Papers

Printed material from the papers of Malcolm MacFarlane (1883-1930), including miscellaneous concert programmes. HP4.89.319

Middlesbrough

Middlesbrough Musical Union
Concert programmes (1908-13) H2.77.75

Paterson and Sons

33 concert programmes (1899-1910) H3.78.410

Paterson's orchestral concerts

Programmes (1887-1931) Mus.Box.250
NE.11.g.5(2-3)
T.358.a

Sunderland

Sunderland Philharmonic Society
Concert programmes (1888-93) AB.2.77.3

Tokyo

Musashino Ongaku Daigaku
Musashino Academia Musicae, Tokyo P.la.3638
Programmes (1961-95, wanting 1971-72, 1978-80, 1984-87, 1991-92)

National Library of Ireland

Charles Acton Collection

Senior music critic for the *Irish Times* (1955-86). Collection contains a broad and representative selection of programmes relating to mostly Dublin events from the 1950s to the 1980s. Items are arranged alphabetically under names of societies, festivals and venues (listed below), and then chronologically within these categories. There are also a number of miscellaneous programmes shelved alphabetically and a selection of programmes from foreign festivals.

Belfast Festival
Belfast College of Music (1963-84) and College Singers (1963-76)
Belfast Concert & Assembly Hall Ltd. (1961-65)
Cork International Choral & Folk Dance Festival (1972-84)
Culwick Choral Society (1960-84)
Dublin Arts Festival (1970-79)
Dublin Festival of 20th Century Music (1970-84)
Dublin Grand Opera Society (1958-70, 1971-79, 1970-78, 1979-85)
Dublin International Festival of Music & the Arts (1960-61)
Dun Laoghaire Summer Festival (1976-86)
Feis Ceoil Prizewinners Concerts (1962-85)
Festival in Great Irish Houses (1978-85)
Gaiety Theatre (Rathmines, Rathgar Musical Society) (1960-81)
German (Goethe) Institute (1970-85)
Istituto Italiano di Cultura Dublin (1960-85)
Killarney Bach Festival
Kilkenny Arts Week (1974-77, 1978-85)
Music Association of Ireland (1963-85)
National Concert Hall (1981-82, 1983, 1984, 1985, 1986)
New Irish Chamber Orchestra (1970-85)
RTÉ Symphony Orchestra (1960-84)
RTÉ Light Orchestra (1978-85)
RTÉ Singers (1965-82)
RTÉ String Quartet (1969-79)
RTÉ Whats On? (1968-70)
RDS Recitals (1960-71, 1972-80, 1981-85)
Royal Irish Academy (1959-85)
St. Ann's Church Dawson St (1966-76, 1976-85)
St. James's Gate Musical Society (1964-65, 1967-69, 1970-83)
Summer Music at Carrolls (1976-85)
Tostal Corcai (1958-64)
University of Dublin Choral Society (1960-79)
Wexford Opera Festival

Joseph Holloway Collection

Joseph Holloway was best known as an aficionado of all aspects of Dublin theatrical life. The collection also includes his vast accumulation of ephemeral items such as programmes, playbills and prompt-sheets. Much of this material is held in the Ephemera Department of the National Library and a project is currently underway to sort, list and improve access to the collection. Queries regarding the Holloway concert programmes project can be directed to the Ephemera Librarian.

Miscellaneous Programmes

The National Library of Ireland holds miscellaneous concert programmes from the nineteenth and twentieth centuries. The following list represents a selection of the holdings. Researchers should consult the library's online catalogue and card catalogues for further examples.

- 1st Dublin Grand Musical Festival (1831), featuring Paganini
- Recitals at the Antient Concert Rooms (1840s)
- Recitals of the Dublin Madrigal Society (1840s)
- Dublin Orchestral Society (1890s-1910s) conducted by Michele Esposito
- Sunday Orchestral Concerts (1905-14) at the Antient Concert Rooms conducted by Michele Esposito
- Royal Dublin Society Concert Programmes (1880s-1920s), largely chamber music with notes by Robert Stewart and Ebenezer Prout
- Cork Orchestral Society (1935-60)
- Programmes for music festivals including Feis Ceoil, Father Mathew Feis, Larne Music Festival and Sligo Feis Ceoil

Other societies and venues including: Abbey Theatre; Belfast Philharmonic Society; Chamber Music Union; Dublin Musical Society; Hallé Concert Society; Hallé Orchestra; Royal Academy Musical Union; Theatre Royal; University of Dublin Choral Society.

Index